THE MAN WHO CRIED

THE MAN WHO CRIED
Sally Potter

faber and faber
LONDON·NEW YORK

First published in 2000
by Faber and Faber Limited
3 Queen Square London WC1N 3AU
Published in the United States by Faber and Faber Inc.
an affiliate of Farrar, Straus and Giroux, New York

Photoset by Faber and Faber Ltd
Printed in England by Mackays of Chatham plc, Chatham, Kent

A CIP record for this book
is available from the British Library

ISBN 0–571–20748–0

2 4 6 8 10 9 7 5 3 1

CONTENTS

ACKNOWLEDGEMENTS

I have been blessed with an exceptional crew and cast for this film, and innumerable allies behind the scenes. For their contribution in the development period, I would like to thank in particular Diane Balser for reading an early draft and clarifying many issues about Jewish history, and Isabel Fonseca for educating me about the history of the Gypsies and generously sharing her contacts and researches with me; Julie Christie for reading the script aloud to me at a crucial moment; Robyn Davidson, Hervé Schneid and Osvaldo Golijov for their intelligent comments and criticisms; Walter Donohue for his endurance, freshness and astute commentaries during endless revisions from start to finish; and Amos Field Reid for his enthusiastic typing and tactful support way beyond the call of duty. Finally, I would like to thank Christopher Sheppard who, once again, gave me the great gift of belief that it was all possible and supported the development of this film from the first seedling of the idea, through to its realization, with energy, dedication and courage.

Sally Potter.

INTRODUCTION

A screenplay is a living thing. It's hard to say when it's 'finished'. Perhaps not until the first real audience watches the film. And even then the public seems to write it anew – each individual in his or her own way. Certainly critics then re-invent what the film means and their view circulates as a version of its reality. And of course there are interviews, in which the film-maker tries to figure out what he or she has done, which may depart radically from the original script.

Why does a screenplay seem to have such mutability? Because it must. The process of making a film (and the making of it begins from the first seedling of an idea to the last check of the final print – and perhaps beyond if one includes checking projection conditions) involves a complex negotiation between dream and reality, imagination and pragmatism. If the writer/director sticks rigidly to an ideal vision of what the film must look like, sound like, and even what the characters should say to each other, not only may the film not get made, but also a great opportunity is missed – the chance to incorporate interesting accidents, the skills and input of the crew, the strange and unpredictable realities that the circumstances of the preparation and shoot offer up, and the unique qualities that each actor brings to a film.

The key seems to be to know when to be open and flexible enough to depart from the original idea – to see each change as a welcome evolution and improvement – and when to hold true and fight fiercely for a vision that perhaps no one else understands (and indeed to accept that no one else may understand until the film is complete and all the elements of the jigsaw are in place).

In my case, as a writer/director, I have the opportunity – which can be both a blessing and a curse – to rewrite perpetually during the working process without referring to another 'authority' – the writer. Nevertheless, the director in me (who also 'writes' through the creation of the *mise-en-scène*) must respect the writer in me who has worked so long and so thoroughly on the script. But there is a simple question that must always be asked: Does it work? And if not, why not? I have found that symptoms of malaise appear during preparation and shooting that simply won't go away until the problem is dealt with at script level. The problem can *appear* to be one of design or costume – for example, you simply cannot figure out what the character should be wearing for a particular scene. On closer examination you realize that the scene has been set at the wrong time of day, or in the wrong place, or indeed shouldn't be there at all. The scissors come out. But if you know that the screenplay you have spent month upon month refining can be changed or cut at a moment's notice under the stressful, pressurized conditions of a shoot, what real status does it have?

It has the status of an imaginary body. It needs to have a sound skeletal structure – one which allows it to move – a complex set of internal functions, and a good heart. Then it must be fleshed out and have a containing outward appearance that holds it all together. And, dare I say it, a soul. The screenwriter sits in isolation (usually), working on all these levels: testing, analyzing, intuiting; feeling for each of the characters, researching in the outer world and in his or her own bank of experience. Eventually, a document is arrived at that must hold its own from multiple points of view. It must be technically able to serve as a blueprint for design and location research; each character must be well enough drawn and sufficiently rich in contradiction and complexity for an actor to have something challenging to work with; and it must be dramatically sound enough to withstand shooting out of sequence, in fragments, and still emerge in the cutting-room with a correct sense of pace and development. It must also be able to withstand awkward questions from everyone from the script supervisor, the hair and make-up team, to the focus-puller ('Which part of the frame should be in focus?' Not always an easy question to answer.)

So the screenwriter (especially if she or he is also the director) has the task of thinking through all these things in advance, when there is the time and space to be contemplative, cerebral, to drift in reverie, to laugh and cry with the characters, to ask the big philosophical questions, like – why? what does it mean? – and the apparently small ones, like – should this scene be set in the morning or the evening?

And then there is the question of responsibility. A film can be seen by millions of people, held captive for an hour and a half or so of their precious existence. I find that increasingly I ask myself what I am adding to their lives.

My own favourite cinematic experiences are when I feel that the film-maker has somehow helped me to 'wake up' through the world that he or she has created. I feel then a strange clarity, as if I have had a glimpse of a hidden order, an underlying meaning, which otherwise might have eluded me. I feel recognized, as if in the frame of light a part of me has found form. And this I'm sure is a consequence of the conceptual and actual framing, in both the script and direction, by the authors of the film.

A film is the end result of multiple choices, first of subject matter and then of how it is realized. Choices that are based on the premise of trying to generate hope, truth and rightness seem more useful than those perpetuating despair and meaninglessness. Sometimes, of course, the truth is ugly. Pain and confusion proliferate everywhere. To pretend otherwise would negate most people's experience. Nevertheless, there is a choice of point of view about the meaning of suffering. It seems that the bigger the frame of reference one uses when looking at any phenomenon, the more likely one is to find some clarity about it. So this is what I aim for: to look at something specific, but with a field of vision that implies a transcendent principle, and which therefore generates hope (itself a form of awakening). I am conscious of failing in the attempt, but I would rather try and fail than not try at all.

In the case of the particular subject matter of *The Man Who Cried* I faced further responsibilities. I was dealing with a moment in history before my own lifetime and with cultures I am not a part of. I am neither Jewish nor a Gypsy. I am not Russian or Italian. I am not a man. But perhaps I am a little bit of all these things (perhaps we all are). Certainly, in order to write the characters I needed to identify with them and their struggles; to understand them and love them equally.

I think part of the attraction (if I can call it that) of the subject matter was that I grew up under its shadow. I remember indelibly the moment when, as a young child, I found out about the holocaust. I stumbled across details of the concentration camps on a sheet of greasy newspaper that some fish and chips were wrapped in. I wept and wept in terror and incomprehension, imagining what I might have done in the place of those incarcerated; could I have escaped, somehow? Could I have survived? And why, how could some human beings do such terrible things to others? All these years later I think *The Man Who Cried* is part of my attempt to look at these issues; the fear of difference as the basis for persecution, the slide into betrayal for some, and the question of survival for others. However, as the Second World War is now familiar to most people and the iconography of the holocaust is in danger of becoming pornographic, I decided to set this story just *before* its horrors and to have the heroine always one step ahead of disaster.

This was to be a film where history was not in your face – nor violence, nor military destruction. The scale of events was to be human, personal. The struggles would be those we all face every day – the struggles for friendship, for work and money, for love. And then, little by little, the choices the characters would make under the pressure of the threat of war – the necessity to take sides – would define who and what they were.

I wanted to draw the characters in such a way that we would be enchanted by them all, including the 'bad' or inadequate ones, and would understand and identify with their struggles.

Perhaps because the subject was 'heavy', I felt the need for the story to be told in a light, energetic way, with elliptical movement through space and time; liberal use of irony and humour; and a primary role for music, from the soaring tenor arias of Italian opera to the haunting, rhythmically charged music of the Romany people. Music holds a key place for all immigrants. It's an expression of the soul of a people, a reminder of who you are, and where you came from. A voice in song can express truth and longing more clearly than in everyday language. The longing to be connected, the longing to transcend pain and oppression, the longing for joy and for love. The intention was to find a way of telling the story where music was carrying emotional and spiritual truth with as much force as the image, the *mise-en-scène* and the characters. The parallels in the history of oppression of the Gypsies and the Jews was to be the subtext shaping the dynamic of the relationship between the heroine, Suzie, and her lover, Cesar. Some of the characters would talk with words, but Suzie and

Cesar would talk with silences. And music would talk for all of them.

I first wrote a draft of *The Man Who Cried* in the period following the release of *Orlando* (1993). I decided, however, to put it aside for *The Tango Lesson*. I didn't feel ready to take on such a big subject. I wanted to get it right, and, besides, I could not resolve some of the narrative problems. When I returned to work on it (in 1997) I decided to try another tack. I put the screenplay aside and sat down to write it as a short story – to let the narrative and characters go where they needed to without thought of 'scenes' or other technical demands.

When I had completed the short story to my satisfaction, I then set about adapting it, almost as if someone else had written it. This proved an extremely productive and interesting way to work. In its long evolution the script changed in many ways. Cesar at one time was a Spanish anarchist. Suzie joined the resistance in a subplot that would have made the film extremely long. The ending changed innumerable times – her father was already dead, or living in poverty in New York. Madame Goldstein was a spy. Lola went to Hollywood. And so on. But the storyline gradually settled into its current form.

The heroine, Suzie, is always one step ahead of disaster – she is 'lucky' but she is also lost, driven into silence as her language (Yiddish) is taken away, re-finding her voice through song. Where Suzie is the singer who is silent, Lola is the dancer who talks incessantly. Lola was based on many such Russian women I met during research trips for *Orlando* and where I learnt so much about different strategies for female survival East and West. With Dante Dominio I intended to develop the paradox of how beauty and weakness (or corruption) can coexist in one body. How can such a beautiful voice come from such a character? Cesar is the conduit into the world of the Gypsies, where Suzie once again contacts a culture where family and community are still alive, and where their aliveness is also communicated through music.

And then the casting initiated its own subtle changes. Working with such splendid, skilled, intelligent actors was an opportunity to learn and improve upon what I had written. A good actor asks difficult, pertinent questions. He or she must be able to make sense of what they are doing. Dialogue is the least of it. Motivation, and the orchestration of the inner life of the character, whether it manifests in a word, an action, a gesture or a look, is what counts. Each of the actors added immeasurably to their character, for which I am grateful.

A word about fathers. The through line in this story is Suzie's search for her father. His absence haunts her life. During the writing process I found myself contemplating the absent father. My own life, and that of many of my friends, was shadowed by our fathers' absence. I came to realize that this was a big part of the twentieth-century story. The World Wars plucked men from their families and often destroyed them. In some cultures, persecution and emigration separated many men from their loved ones; whilst in others, divorce and working patterns took men from their children. Perhaps we are all, to some degree, mourning our missing fathers. We are living with a legacy of men separated not just from their families but perhaps even from themselves. This is a deep grief.

Which brings us to the title of the film, *The Man Who Cried*. In the story it is not one man who cries, but several, and we witness their tears through Suzie's eyes. But a cry is also another word for the voice in song, celebrating and expressing in music that which cannot be expressed any other way. So, interwoven in the story are the musical strands which express cultural difference and universal sentiment – struggle, loss, love, betrayal, friendship – both through so-called 'high art' and 'popular culture', the voices of insiders and outsiders; each with a reminder of our commonality.

Sadly, the lessons of the Second World War don't seem to have been learnt. Difference is still a reason for persecution. Nationalism, scape-goating and 'ethnic cleansing' all continue in various guises. My hope is that this film may be able to function as a 'voice' for those who were (and are) silenced; mourn those who were lost; and celebrate the survival of those who lived.

THE MAN WHO CRIED –
STORY

This is the story written as described in the Introduction. It was then adapted (and changed) until it became the script that follows.

My little bird, says the tall thin man, smiling. Fegele.

She is waving her arms like wings as she sits on his shoulders high above the world, shrieking with vertigo and pleasure as he strides out, the long, confident steps of a man who knows where he is going.

Fegele, my Fegele. He sings to her, his little bird, in his deep, sonorous voice, a voice of joy which finds its echo above his head in her laughing face framed ecstatically against the endless blue summer sky.

Everyone in the shtetl, a small dilapidated town near Minsk, knows how this father delights in his little daughter, and tolerates more than he should, out of love and relief that she is his, and that she is alive. She won't sit still or be quiet, say the older women, but it's understandable. She was born on the move after all, crossing the border. To be born like that, in the back of a cart, the shouts of the men driving the horses on, faster and faster, and the screams of her mother and what can you expect? A motherless child and she's still running. How he loves her, and who wouldn't? But later on, how will anyone be able to control such a child?

The years pass as they always have since these people were confined to The Pale, the area designated for Jews within the vast Russian landscape. The men study and the women work. There's very little money, but there's usually enough to eat, although now even food is becoming scarce. Everyone knows everyone, and everyone argues, with each other and with God. And at night the candles are lit and the entire community crowds noisily into the synagogue. The children run ragged and barefoot between the adults' legs as they talk and pray.

But when the tall thin man starts to sing, the raucous, murmuring crowd is silenced. The little girl stops running too, looks up at her father and then at the familiar faces all around, as they drink in his voice, soothed, calmed and fortified. Ah, she's so proud of him.

And then, one day, a prodigal son returns to the fold. Someone who left the shtetl, who joined the ever-growing exodus across the sea to a place where all men are equal and all men are free and money is there to be earned if you're young and willing. But this son has returned to show off his wealth and collect his betrothed.

He's wearing a suit, a shiny blue suit, and a hat. Not the fur hat of the men of the shtetl, but a racy hat at a jaunty angle. He hands out sweets and toys to the children who cluster around him. Mr Money they call him as they dig in his pockets for more; the richest man in the world.

Suddenly the men of the shtetl look shabby and dark in their traditional long black coats. What was cosy and familiar seems musty and inferior. There's a choking, aching envy in the breasts of the young men.

And then there's a wedding; a blushing bride, excited beyond measure; weeping parents, who know they will never see their daughter again. And the tall thin man sings for them all – a song of joy for the young married couple – a song with a sob in the throat for a way of life that is about to be left behind for ever.

After the happy couple have gone the shtetl returns to normal. But it is pervaded by restlessness. There is a word, a new word, on everybody's lips. America, America. It's like a prayer, a litany for the living, a promise for a future that had all but been forgotten in the struggle to maintain a present based on the past. And now the rumours are growing of incidents of violence not so far away.

Poverty was bearable. But now the scape-goating, the random acts of cruelty, the pointed finger, the glaring, hostile faces of peasants and revolutionaries alike . . . What is to be done?

One night the little girl is lying in her bed when she hears raised voices in the kitchen – and that word again – and the pleading tones of her grandmother and then her father shouting.

She stands half-naked, barefoot, in the doorway, watching and listening, bewildered. Her father turns and sees her, scoops her up in his arms, and takes her back to bed. Fegele, my little Fegele, he croons, comfortingly, stroking her brow, singing to her in his lovely deep voice, a lullaby, his special lullaby for her.

But in the harsh daylight not so many weeks later, she is clinging to his legs, screaming, as he tries to leave. A small group of men stand waiting, impatiently, their bags tied to their backs.

The tall thin man stands staring down helplessly at his grief-racked tiny daughter, drinking her in with his eyes full of tears which course silently down his cheeks.

The girl's grandmother uncurls the child's fingers one by one from their furious grip, murmuring words with all the conviction she can muster – he will send for us, let him go, you must let him go now, let your father go.

But in the evening when the two of them sit in front of their bowls of cabbage soup, immobile, as the darkness folds itself around them, the old woman is silent.

In the months that follow the little girl is wilder than ever. It is she who leads the games the children play in the fields and forests around the shtetl. It's always the same game. Someone is leaving, and someone is being left behind. Bags are packed (an old box, a scrap of cloth), food is handed over for the journey (some grass or leaves), goodbyes are said, and then the emigrant is gone. Depending on the day, and the mood of the children, he may return (from behind a tree, or from the deep, waving grass). Mr Money, with his pockets bulging and his jaunty hat.

One day, it is the little girl whose turn it is to leave in this endlessly repeatable game. She runs into the forest, away, far away from the two little boys she has so cruelly abandoned. Farther than she has ever run before. Suddenly she's alone in the green light of the pines, alone with the tall trees.

But then she hears a sound.

She crouches, and she watches.

A young boy, dark-skinned, colourfully dressed, leading a horse. He's teasing the horse this way and that, the two of them lost in a quiet communion.

And then behind him, more horses, caravans, a group of Gypsies on the move on the path through the forest.

When the little girl rejoins her friends, breathless, under cover of the long, waving grass, she's forgotten to be Mr Money. But in any case, they have forgotten too, because they are lying on their stomachs staring at the horizon, at the columns of black smoke snaking into the sky.

And then the shouts of their mothers – higher than usual, more urgent than usual – call them out of their reverie.

Shouts, cries, chaos, the old woman's hands shaking as she empties the jar of sugar in the cupboard on to the table, scrabbles for the three gold coins hidden there, and then with trembling fingers sews the coins into the lining of her granddaughter's coat.

Three men standing at the door, the older one and his two adolescent sons, their fur hats, their pale faces; the old woman's voice pleading with the men, pressing food upon them, bread, cheese, precious meat; and then pressing the child upon them too and that word – America – like a curse or a prayer; and last of all, as the child is handed up to the men on top of the cart, the old woman runs back into the house, reaches up, and tears down the framed photo of the child's father – formal, posed and already fading; pious, upright, a tall, thin, religious-looking man – and thrusts the photo into the child's arms with bread, more bread, and lamentation.

And so the journey begins that takes the little girl and the three men further than any of them have ever been before, across steppe and through forests, through the smouldering remains of what were villages, as they cut a path across country, through the devastation of the civil war, towards the border. The child lies on top of the bundles of possessions on the cart, looking out with dark eyes and listening to everything, the swaying backs of the three men in their fur hats before her, and the swallowing night behind her.

She wakes alone in the cold, frosty darkness, on top of the cart, near the border. She can hear raised voices coming from the hut at the side of the road.

And then, incomprehensibly, they've left their horse and cart behind and are walking away from the road, carrying their wretched possessions on their backs, and the older man is carrying more. He is carrying some bundles he's been made to carry by the men in the hut through the icy fields at night. The little girl is still clutching the photo her grandmother gave her, although the frame has long since been abandoned, the glass shattered.

And then they reach the road again on the other side of the border after their tortuous circumnavigation, and it's shouts, and lights, and the older man is taken, along with the heavy bundles that were not his, by men in uniform. But he had instructed his sons to stay back in the shadows, just in case anything should happen to him, and then to continue, come what may, and to take the girl, and never to look back, do you hear?

And so the little girl and the two adolescent boys in their fur hats walk, and sometimes ride, in a car! a car! with headlights that pick out the cows standing ghost-like by the side of the road, until they reach a place that's called a port, with dark, dark water that seems to stretch away for ever.

And there, more hands, and words, and the boys bending down to cut the gold coins out of the child's coat, and then she's handed over, yes, to America, because that is where her boat is going, just like yours, says the fat man with the strange smile, to the two young men in their fur hats as they disappear with an anxious wave.

Sickness, dark, and the bodies of strangers. It's an inferno, a swaying, tossing hell in the hold of the ship that ends in the cold grey light of another country where men speak in strange, harsh voices in a babbling tongue they call English.

America, this is America, say the desperate, weary voices all around her. Except that it's not.

And the little girl is one of a group of children alone, lined up against a wall, being inspected – for lice, for disease – for foreign and unnameable maladies of all kinds.

And then a portly man carrying a clipboard is passing down the line giving each child the gift of a pronounceable name.

When he reaches the little girl with dark eyes, still clutching the remains of the photo, he bends down and looks into her face. Suzie, he says, for a black-eyed Susan, in his northern English accent. She looks up at him, stilled and silenced by exhaustion, by the endless sickness, by the terrors of abandonment, and now by bafflement at the incomprehensible sounds coming out from the red cavernous mouth beneath his bristly grey moustache.

It seems she has arrived.

The child is passed from uniformed hand to uniformed hand, from bus to train and finally into the care of a lady with virulent red hair and a tight, anxious smile, her ghostly husband hovering in the background.

The lady's smile never falters as the only possession the child has is finally pulled from her fingers and taken from her, for her own good, mind, because it will only make her upset. And then she is plunged into a bath – huge, steaming, white, antiseptic – and scrubbed clean, cleaner than clean. There, that's better then, Suzie, isn't it?

The room that the little girl finds herself in is cold and alien. A heavy dark wardrobe, a high narrow bed, a swirling floral carpet, long fussy curtains framing the high window. And, hanging above the bed like a warning, a tiny crucifix, Jesus, in agony, nailed to the cross.

The girl sits perched on the edge of the bed in an oversized candlewick dressing-gown, tartan slippers with pom-poms dwarfing her tiny feet, and stares silently about her. It's a silence that she wears like armour.

At school, in the playground, the other children cluster around her, pointing and poking at her, curious and casually hostile, with the learned distrust of the foreigner, as she fails to respond to their interrogations.
    Where are you from?
    She don't know.
    She's a Gypsy. Gypsy!

But Suzie utters not a word.

And then in the classroom, when she is pulled to the front of the class and told to count out loud, one two three, the shiny conkers hanging on strings: silence.

And then at the outdoor municipal baths, when the children, purple with cold, are told to stand in crocodile formation in the water, three of them hold Suzie down, in the shallow end, just to see if it will make her speak when she comes spluttering, red-faced, to the surface; but no, she just stands there, gasping, with a wild look about her.

And then, finally, when the lady with virulent red hair finds Suzie in the front room in the middle of the night – the front room with its dust covers on the three-piece suite and its ornaments on the mantelpiece and its framed photos of Mr and Mrs Red Hair at their wedding now smashed on the floor – and the lady slaps her, but Suzie doesn't cry, just stares up with dark eyes flaming – her silence has become absolute.

The doctor claps behind her right ear and Suzie jumps. He peers into her ears, his stethoscope dangling.

He looks into her throat.

He bangs her back, suddenly, and makes her cough and cry out.

And then he stares at her kindly.

There's nothing wrong with the child. Just give her time, he says.

And then, one day in the asphalt playground, in the morning break, the children are clustering at the gates, peering out.

Tinkers!

Suzie looks out, too, at the boy leading the horse, the caravan, the women in their bright clothes carrying baskets full of clothes pegs.

And when the other children have returned to their play – to skipping games and jacks and marbles and fights – Suzie is still staring through the gates at the figures as they disappear into the distance. But now she is singing, quietly, a song to herself, in Yiddish, her native tongue.

But someone is listening. The teacher on playground duty has heard the dark, dumb girl singing. And he takes it upon himself to teach this girl to speak, to speak English, by getting her to sing. He keeps her back, alone, after school and makes her sing tunes; any tunes will do at first; and then hymns, real hymns, with English words. And he punishes her, but kindly, every time she lapses into Yiddish.

All things bright and beautiful, all creatures great and small.
On and on, over and over.
All things bright and beautiful, the Lord God made them all.

And so, little by little, Suzie learns to sing, to speak English and to forget.

She forgets her first language, she forgets where she came from, but she does not forget where she's going. When the teacher asks the children what they will be when they grow up and the boys answer: fireman, teacher, doctor; and the girls: mother, teacher, nurse; Suzie says that when she grows up she will be an American.
And they laugh.

But when her teacher proudly puts Suzie on the little stage in the assembly hall and gets her to sing to the school, accompanied by the mousy school pianist, the restless children become quiet. The teacher stands listening at the back of the hall in his tweed suit, his arms folded across his chest, and his eyes fill with tears as her pure, high voice soars out across the sea of heads.

Afterwards, in the playground, Suzie is invited to join in the skipping games with the other girls, though some of them imitate her singing, enviously, behind her back, and call her teacher's pet, and then imitate the teacher's tears that he had thought unseen.

And so she discovers that her tool of survival – her singing voice – is a blessing but also a curse. Some will love her for what she can do, but some will hate her for it, too. So she learns to parody herself for the other children, to pre-empt their mockery, to win friends where otherwise she would find only rivals. And she learns to hold part of herself back. Even when she is playing, noisily, with the other girls, the core of her is silent, watchful, waiting.

Waiting to resume the journey she had once begun but never completed.

So at the first opportunity she takes the first step. Encouraged by the mousy piano accompanist, watched sadly by the tweedy teacher who privately hoped one day to make her his wife, she sets off for her first audition when she comes of age; old enough to leave school, old enough to earn a living, though not yet old enough to vote.

She leaves the house that was never home and says goodbye to the lady with virulent red hair and her silent, almost invisible husband lurking in the background (the man who had crept so often into her bedroom at night and endlessly whispered to her of his loneliness, long before she could understand a word he said, and then had reached out to touch her, making her promise over and over to never leave him, never, now that he had his very own little girl), and as she goes the shred of photo is, at last, returned to her. The photo of her father that was taken from her for her own good and held in safe-keeping for this very day.

Alone in the hostel for chorus girls that she finds herself in that night, she stares at the photo, at the tall thin man standing to attention for the camera, as if she is hypnotized by a ghost.

Why did you leave me? Why? She whispers.
  What did I do wrong?
  And then she slumps, listless, paralysed by amnesia and confusion.

But on stage – dressed as a banana, or a tree (because she's an in-between height and will do as a stand-in when one of the show-girls is sick), or kicking her legs in the can-can (because she's slim and fit and more or less gets her legs up) or singing in the heavenly choir number dressed in nothing but a pair of wings – she works hard and gets noticed and is amongst the lucky few from Miss Modern's Touring Troupe who are chosen to go to Paris.
  Paris – gateway to Europe, gateway to the world, a step in the right direction, says Miss Modern with her fearsome enthusiasm, if you want to get to America, dear. Contacts to be made, money to be earned, money to be saved, and who knows.

Her room in Paris is small but light, high up amongst the rooftops, with windows that open on to the sky. It's a tall building that once was grand but now is a shabby rabbit warren of rooms and apartments. The concierge in the musty rooms on the ground floor sees everything and says nothing; but sometimes there's a familiar smell coming from her kitchen: the smell of cabbage soup.

Suzie works at night and sleeps late in the day and wears her coat indoors and eats cheap sausage from the market so that she can put most of what she earns into a jar of sugar in the cupboard above the sink behind the screen in the corner of her tiny room.

One night Suzie wakes, alone in her room, sweating, to the sound of shouts and screams and breaking glass. But when she steps out on to the little balcony she sees only the twinkling stars in the velvety sky above the peaceful, sleeping rooftops.

And after a few weeks Suzie finds that here, at last, in Paris, she feels safe and she can breathe a little, and so something in her starts to let go.

When she walks along the boulevards with her friends from the chorus there's a jaunty swing in her stride, the way a young woman walks who has a room of her own, and is prepared to turn her hand to almost anything to earn a few extra francs to add to her savings. So when Miss Modern's troupe returns to England, she decides to stay.

It's her friend Lola, the dancer from Russia, voluble, voluptuous and full of blonde ambition, who always knows what jobs are going, and who to talk to to get them. Before long, Lola, who never seems to have any money in her pocket and is always falling behind with her rent – because a beauty like her must have clothes, new clothes, or she is nothing – has moved in with Suzie. So now there are two beds in the tiny room at the top of the world.

Two beds and a Christmas tree, that frosty December in 1938. A tree that they have carried home between them through the wintry streets, laughing, after Lola finds Suzie standing amongst the forest of Christmas trees in the market, her eyes closed, breathing in the scent of pine, a look of rapture on her face.

It is later that night that Lola discovers that Suzie must have come from Russia, too, from the lettering on the back of the scrap of photo that Suzie shyly shows her. The address of the studio in the town where the photograph was taken, and a man's name written beside it, are virtually illegible, but are unmistakably in Russian script, Cyrillic.

Lola becomes excited when she finally deciphers the address, and starts to chatter away in Russian, but in vain, because Suzie understands not a word. Lola stares at the photo, at the clothes the tall thin man is wearing, and quietly repeats the man's name.

Ah, but so, she says, he was a Jew.

It is at a party – a glittering party, for the glamorous people of Paris with money to spend and an insatiable appetite for the arts – where Suzie and Lola are working for the evening, posing in next to nothing in a tableau on either side of a jewelled horse, as the chattering guests laugh and talk around them (and about them, as if they were deaf), that they both meet the men who will change their lives.

Silence, silence, everyone. Tonight we're so lucky to have with us the new guest star of the opera, Dante Dominio, and he has agreed to give us just a taste, a little taste . . .

And when this tall, elegant man steps forward, throws back his head, and starts to sing, Lola stares and slowly smiles. But Suzie begins to tremble, uncontrollably, like the horse beside her. The dark man sitting so still on the horse between the two women watches them both. He strokes the twitching neck of his horse, and then reaches out, instinctively, and puts a hand on Suzie's neck too, to quieten her, to soothe her trembling.

It is Lola, later, who manoeuvres her way through the crowd towards Dante, pulling Suzie behind her, and who manages, somehow, to catch his attention with her flashing smile, and who manages also, somehow, to tell him that she is a dancer who needs a job and asks him can he help; and out of largesse, and because he feels flattered to be needed by such a beauty, he waves her towards the hovering grey-haired man from the opera house, who reluctantly agrees to audition her; and then it's not just the blonde, but her dark friend, too, because she can sing, really, she has a lovely voice you know.

And so, from being dressed as fruit or draped in feathers on small stages in seedy revues or at glamorous parties, the two girls find themselves dressed as Valkyries in the new Wagnerian production at the opera. It's a grand production, with sound effects and heavy romantic scenery in the German style, and horses, real horses, that charge across a ramp at the back of the stage, ridden by three young men wearing long flaxen wigs and winged helmets.

Two of the men are boys, really, young, dark-skinned boys; but the third, the one in charge of them and of the horses, is Cesar, the quiet man from the party who had reached out to soothe Suzie's trembling.

Little by little Lola moves into Dante's orbit, working her charms relentlessly, ruthlessly, now that her goal is clear. She pulls Suzie in her wake as a dark foil to her clear-skinned beauty.

And because Suzie is under the spell of Dante's soaring voice, she gladly tags along, sitting in the back of his chauffeur-driven car as they speed along the boulevards at night after the performance, watching with admiration, astonishment, and a little envy, as Lola laughs and flatters her way ever closer to the man she wants and must have.

But this man with the glorious voice has a way of speaking, a way of thinking, that jars. He worships the strong and despises the weak. One night when he gets out of his car a Gypsy beggar child wraps himself around his elegant leg like a limpet and Dante angrily shakes him off like a fly. He defends his pride as others might defend their principles, and misses no opportunity, whether sitting in a fashionable night-club or gliding in a boat along the Seine, to air his opinions about world events. The Germans are right to take Poland, he says, just as the Italians were right to take Albania. Mussolini is his man, a man's man, a man who understands the needs of the Italian people for dignity, the needs of the nation for respect. And so on.

And at the theatre Dante misses no opportunity to jibe at the dark-skinned, nationless horsemen waiting in the wings. Lola giggles at his jokes, but Suzie remains silent.

But they're Gypsies, don't you see, says Lola.

Just Gypsies.

From that moment on Suzie no longer tags along with Lola, but prefers to watch as Cesar and his two friends, or cousins, or brothers, it's not clear which, exercise their horses in the yard behind the theatre.

They don't mix much with the stagehands, the carpenters or the chorus girls, these Gypsy horsemen. They keep themselves to themselves, speaking in Romany with each other. Cesar is the linguist and the spokesman, translating for the younger men when necessary, making sure they're paid as they should be, in money, real money, at the end of each week.

But Cesar gradually breaks his silence to speak with the dark-eyed, watchful Suzie, and after a while he shows her some of what he can *really* do with his horse; riding bareback, teasing the horse this way and that, in small, prancing, dancing steps; a quiet and subtle communion of man and beast.

Then one night, after the show, when Dante has teased Suzie for being a dark horse herself and asks her what she can possibly see in men who prefer to talk to horses rather than women, Cesar takes Suzie along with him to hear his musician friends, or brothers, or cousins, it's not clear which, playing in one of the fashionably crowded cafés. Cesar watches Suzie's glowing face as she listens with all her being to their fast, ecstatic music, whilst the chattering crowds around her listen with only half an ear.

And afterwards Suzie lies at night in the darkness trying not to listen to Lola and Dante's love-making in the narrow bed on the other side of their tiny room. The room that Dante likes to visit because it reminds him of a way of life he left behind a long time ago when he and his mother and his little sisters all lived together in poverty and proximity, in one room, as southern Italian migrants must do in the cold, inhospitable North.

And then Suzie hears how Dante softly weeps as he whispers all of this to Lola when he has come and lies crumpled, small and vulnerable again in Lola's arms.

One day, when the concierge asks Suzie, grumpily, if soon there will be not one, not two, not three, but perhaps four occupants in the little room tonight and then exclaims irritably in Yiddish,

Suzie freezes, rooted to the spot, and suddenly remembers. She asks the concierge to say it again, that word, which she does willingly, and more, though it's no use, because it's only the first exclamation that Suzie remembers, imprinted dimly in her memory in her grandmother's panicking voice.

But that's enough for the concierge to understand what's what. From then on she becomes Suzie's conduit into a world of rumour, fear and also, strangely, of reassurance, because she's safe here, now in Paris, she says, for this is the country where they wrote the Declaration of the Rights of Man. The other women in this street can stare as coldly as they like; she's moved on twice and that is enough already; here the Germans will never come, it's the land in the East they want. And anyway you are lucky, child, because you have an English passport and that will take you anywhere, if ever you need to leave in a hurry, God forbid.

Soon after, on a soft day in early autumn, Suzie learns that England and France have reluctantly declared war on Germany. In the dressing-rooms at the Opera that night there is a flurry of anxiety amongst the chorus.

But in the weeks that follow, after everyone has taken a breath, they decide that nothing in their daily lives has really changed, and so they chatter nonchalantly about the 'phoney war'. It was just a gesture, they say. And, in any case, why get involved in other countries' business? Who wants to die for Danzig? And come to that, there must have been a reason for the events in Germany they are beginning to describe so neutrally in the papers, such as 'Kristallnacht', a night of viciously organized destruction last November. These people must have done something to provoke it, surely. And Suzie remembers her dream of broken glass and realizes that then she was afraid, but now is becoming angry.

So angry that when Dante taunts the Gypsies yet again, for being dirty, and then threatens angrily to have them sacked if one of their horses shits on stage again in the middle of his aria, she can no longer hold back but lets out a torrent of rage in the Gypsies' defence that takes Dante aback with its vehemence and forces Lola to take sides and virtually disown her friend completely. But Dante is quite taken with the transformation of the dark, watchful girl into a fighting cat, and backs down with a puzzled and even strangely erotic smile.

And although at first Cesar's pride is wounded by being defended by a woman, he knows that Suzie has saved his job. By doing this she has crossed an invisible line and has finally qualified to be taken back to meet his people. And so that night they ride on his horses to the outskirts of Paris, to a wasteland shocking in its poverty and filth, but where the insides of the tents and caravans are as clean and as ornately decorated as the Gypsies' bodies themselves.

Suzie meets Cesar's sisters or cousins, it's not clear which, and his mother and father and various uncles and other members of their clan. It seems that it's not usual for a stranger to be admitted in this way, especially not a woman, and so she is greeted warily and with some formality. But Cesar explains that she has proved herself to be a friend, an ally they can trust. Food is offered, and when the women take Suzie aside to wash her hands, they take the opportunity to touch her face and clothes as well, and ask her, gently, where are her children? For they all have them, running freely amongst them everywhere. And the women exclaim pityingly when Suzie says she has none, and stare uncomprehendingly when she tells them she has no family either.

After they have all eaten, and the blaring radios have been turned off, and an old toothless man has sung a song in a voice full of longing, Cesar and the two young men mount their horses and gallop in a circle round a fire on the wasteland, and then one by one raise themselves upside down on their galloping horses' necks until they are vertical, feet pointing to the stars, for Suzie and the other women's amusement and for their own exultation.

And later that night, in an abandoned car on the edge of the encampment, when she and Cesar become lovers at last, Suzie feels, at least for those timeless, hungry moments, that she has come home.

And so begins a love affair that consumes Suzie in a way she has never been consumed before. A love affair conducted in the open air, on derelict street corners, or in the long grass near the river.

And little by little Suzie does not wait to be invited, but turns up at the Gypsy camp often enough to be accepted, to a degree, as the strange woman without a family, who is friends with Cesar and perhaps more, no questions asked because one does not interrogate here, it's considered rude, and uncultured, to do so. It's only the *gadjes*, the non-Gypsies, who endlessly ask this and that, trying to pin you down with names and forms and the hated carnet that every Gypsy must carry at all times which says not only who you are and where you are from, but also carries your fingerprints and bodily measurements too.

Some of Cesar's family continue to be wary of Suzie, looking at her with narrowed eyes as if to say, what does she really want? But the others gradually accord her a status which allows her to move relatively freely amongst them: the status of an honorary man (for surely she is not a woman in their sense of the word), or perhaps the status of an orphan, whose unimaginable aloneness deserves their pity.

One day an old woman takes Suzie's hand and starts to tell her fortune but Cesar interrupts angrily, for this is something the Gypsies do for money or to confuse the *gadjes* with nameless fears. They never do it amongst themselves.

As Suzie becomes more and more involved with the Gypsies and their preoccupations, and learns about their taboos and their beliefs, and even, one rainy night, is persuaded to sing for them, she begins, for the first time, to forget where she was going. Whole days go by where she does not pull out the photo of her father and think of America.

Lola watches Suzie as she visibly blooms, and notes that it has nothing to do with the clothes she's wearing, which are as modest as ever.

But the mood is changing in Paris. The phoney war is threatening to become real. But just who is the enemy? The fear and hatred of Communists is greater than the fear and hatred of the Nazis. And the French Nationalists march more confidently in the streets, raising their arms in the fascist salute, voicing out loud an abrasive distrust of the foreigners in their midst.

Now the familiar gossip in the dressing-rooms backstage at the opera is tinged with a veiled hysteria. For amongst the chorus, the principals, and at all levels of management, there are accents which betray origins other than French. In the search for unity and a sense of belonging, the chatter turns to one group they all feel, somehow, the right to exclude. For who controls the pay packets, about which they all like to complain so bitterly, after all? With a name like that he can only be a Jew.

And when this happens Suzie catches Lola's eye, and Lola looks away.

But one night when Suzie climbs the stairs to their room, which Lola now mainly uses as a wardrobe for her ever-growing collection of sparkly gowns, paid for by Dante, she hears Lola's laugh and Dante's too. Something stops her in her tracks, something instinctively makes her creep unheard up the last flight of stairs and stand outside the door, shivering, as she realizes that Lola has pulled out the photo of Suzie's father from its hiding place and that she and Dante are quietly laughing at it together.

Suzie turns and tiptoes away, down to the ground-floor room, where the concierge takes her in without a word and feeds her hot soup because Suzie suddenly looks thin and hungry and cold.

The next day, when Suzie finds she is aching for Cesar's company in the daylight hours and comes looking for him in the harsh winter sun, she eventually finds him in the barbershop near the encampment, engaged in fierce discussion with the Spanish barber. No, he's not a Gypsy, explains Cesar the linguist in answer to Suzie's questions. The barber is a refugee from the Spanish Civil War, one of many here, who cannot find a home now that they have lost their own. Some of his people are in camps, Suzie, at the border, and some are on the run. We are all becoming travellers now.

But Cesar is embarrassed by Suzie's presence and her questions in this all-male preserve and is cold with her. For the first time she feels unwelcome. As they walk away from the barbershop together under the lightly mocking gaze of the other men he explodes in anger and they fight.

And then Suzie discovers, when she asks Cesar angrily why, if she is not welcome here, he will never come to her little room to make love in the warmth of her bed, instead of always in the wrecks of cars or standing up fully clothed by a wall in the shadows, that one of the reasons Cesar is so angry is because he is humiliated by the fact that he cannot stay overnight in the centre of Paris without risk of imprisonment, for by law he and each of his people must inform the police if they leave their encampment for even one night.

It doesn't surprise Suzie when she gets home, just before the hour of the curfew that has been imposed, to find Lola packing her bags to leave the little room they had shared. But what does surprise her is Lola's resentment, and the envy that lies behind it. Envy for a passion that Suzie has clearly found with Cesar and Lola feels she may be losing with Dante, at the very moment that he has finally invited her to live with him in his grand apartment. Who knows, there may be wedding bells, she says in a hollow voice, and why do you criticize me for wanting to look nice and eat well in restaurants with silver and crystal? But I don't, says Suzie, I haven't said a word. You don't need to, says Lola, you and your kind never do.

And then late one morning soon after, when Suzie comes down to buy some milk for her breakfast from the shop on the corner, she realizes something is wrong.

The concierge's window is open, but it's not her grey-haired friend peering out in her familiar irritable way, it's a fat, implacable, middle-aged peroxide blonde.

Where is she? Where is she?, asks Suzie, but the new concierge only shrugs and gestures vaguely, with a closed face, as if to say that the other Madame disappeared in a puff of smoke, just like that, who knows where, but what else can you expect, these foreigners always come and go. And anyway, didn't you know, she was a Communist.

It is only when Suzie questions the children playing at holding each other down in the street outside that she learns that Madame Goldstein was taken away, in the early hours of the morning, by three men in a shiny black car.

Are you a Communist too, Miss?, the children ask her. No, says Suzie, I am a singer.

And then she finds herself feverishly counting her savings hidden in the jar of sugar and, later, queuing at the shipping office along with a crowd of other anxious-looking people with foreign accents, only to be laughed at by the clerk when she reaches the counter. Full, all full, Mademoiselle. The ships to America are full. You are not the only one who wants to get out.

And so Suzie returns to the opera without telling anyone of her fears, and wears her flaxen wig and winged helmet that night on stage as if nothing had changed, until the day when the production comes to an end and Suzie finds herself suddenly out of work.

She could, perhaps, have stayed on in the chorus for the next production, but when Dante invites her into his dressing-room and propositions her (for her resistance to his charms has become a challenge to his pride), she rejects him in no uncertain terms, and then she loses her foothold at the opera entirely.

In the cold spring weeks that follow, Suzie accompanies Cesar and his brothers when they take their horses to parties where the rich and hysterical in their witty couture dresses are helped on to the horses' backs and ride around in circles, shrieking with exaggerated excitement, whilst the Gypsy musicians, ever popular, play on and wildly on. And Suzie is there to collect the coins that the revellers drop into a hat after the rides and music are done. For she has to eat, and this is as good a job as any.

It is at such a party one night, dressed like a Gypsy, that Suzie sees Lola in her finery, on the other side of the room, tightly holding on to Dante's arm as he holds forth to the beauties surrounding him, and as he smiles, charmingly, flirtatiously, at the blonde party hostess.

And then, later, when Suzie is scooping up the horses' droppings from the parquet floor, she feels Dante's breath upon her neck and hears him whisper, So you have found your *métier* at last. And she looks up at his smiling face, so pleased with his own witticism, and she cannot resist saying in English that it's strange how such a glorious voice could come out of someone so full of shit.

In the early hours of the morning, as the party guests begin to drift drunkenly away, a man in a slightly shabby but well-cut white linen suit, who witnessed this little exchange and who has been speaking immaculate French in a loud voice all evening, approaches Suzie and asks her quietly, in equally immaculate English, if she would like to meet for tea sometime.

And because this man has a kindly look to him and an intelligent smile, and perhaps because he vaguely reminds her of someone who used to visit Madame Goldstein, sitting incongruously in his white suit in her stuffy little room, she says yes.

When they meet for tea, this strangely charming man somehow teases Suzie's story out of her, listening attentively and apparently without judgement, and then says, as they get up to leave, If you ever want to be more than just angry, give me a ring.

It is soon after, one lovely morning in May, that the unthinkable happens, the thing that everyone, but everyone, said would never happen, could never happen. The Germans advance through Belgium and then invade northern France.

Suzie rushes to find Cesar. When she arrives at the encampment she finds the place half empty, except for the usual clutch of old women keeping half an eye out for the band of ragged children scampering about wildly amongst the junk, searching for cigarette stubs on the ground and then smoking them; playing at being men and at moving on.

The old women wave and point in various directions in response to Suzie's questions, habitually protecting their men with disinformation, for the older ones still cannot bring themselves to trust this outsider, until eventually Suzie finds her own way by following the sound of singing; the low harmonics of a funeral dirge.

In the line of men walking behind the pall-bearers, who are lurching through the mud carrying a lace-covered coffin (the whole proceedings absent-mindedly observed by the local Gendarmerie, who now have other things on their minds), Suzie finds Cesar, dressed in mourning.

But in the inn they are all headed for, as Suzie crouches in a corner behind Cesar, she finds out that the coffin was empty and that this is the only way the people of all the different Gypsy tribes around Paris could meet undisturbed to decide what to do.

Cesar translates for her in a whisper, now and then, as the men stand up one by one to declare that now is the time to bury their differences and beg each other for forgiveness for real or imagined hostilities, as if they were on their deathbeds each and every one and had no reason any more to hold on to pointless grudges or feuds.

And then the toothless one stands and in his low musical voice utters a long and elaborate curse against anyone who will not stand to defend his kin.

For, as Suzie later discovers from Cesar as they stand in the darkness together on the bridge overlooking the railway tracks near the encampment, other groups of Gypsies have already been interned in camps in the south of France, and it is known that members of their tribes have been imprisoned and killed in terrible, unimaginable circumstances in Poland and Germany.
    The time has come to do something.

You're right, you're right, says Suzie, eagerly, trembling, I agree, me too. I'm with you. But Cesar looks at her gently, and then silently strokes her neck.

The next day the gradual civilian exodus from Paris begins, in cars, on bicycles and on foot. Even the shy student in the room next to Suzie loads his meagre possessions on to his bicycle and leaves for the south.

When Suzie passes a ministry building and joins the curious crowds gathered behind the tall wrought-iron gates watching as officials resignedly burn box after box of government papers in a great bonfire in the courtyard, she remembers the man in the white suit, and what he had said to her as he slipped her his card. And so she calls him on the number he had given her.

And when they meet that afternoon she finds that because she feels safe with this man at the very moment when she is about to put herself in the greatest danger she has ever known, she agrees, quite casually, to try to become a go-between between the Gypsies and the beginnings of the organized resistance which he represents. The man in the white suit draws out what Suzie knows about the Gypsies' way of doing things, helps her see that her perpetual watchfulness has a function, and tells her that because she can move between worlds with more ease than most she will be trusted enough to carry messages, to carry responsibility, when the time comes. And it will come, he says. And suddenly, for the first time since the day that Suzie arrived in England as a child, the fact that she has never really fitted in anywhere appears to her to have a purpose. Not quite English, never visibly a Jew, and now neither French nor a Gypsy, and yet, at times, passably any of these; the chameleon at last has found her place.

Only when they are about to part does Suzie ask him why he lets himself be so conspicuous in his white suit in a job that surely needs to be so secret, and he says: Sometimes it's easier to hide in the spotlight, my dear. But you're a performer, you know all about that.

And so Suzie's love affair with Cesar starts to shift its focus. As the Germans advance inexorably through northern France, and as the mass exodus from Paris continues, the sight of trickling lines of people pushing their possessions on bikes or in prams becoming ever more familiar, the trust that Suzie and Cesar have built becomes a bridge. For the Gypsies' learned and habitual distrust of the outsider which, historically, has ensured their survival, has also ensured their isolation. In these exceptional circumstances something has to change.

The Gypsies' subtle skills need to be nurtured and gradually prepared for action. Their secret system of roadside signs criss-crossing France (and indeed the whole of Europe) is an invaluable potential communication channel for the Resistance. Furthermore, they are expert information gatherers; they often know what is happening across Europe before the population at large, for somebody from their extended family is always travelling with first-hand news. The Gypsies' relative mobility and knowledge of the road will enable them to help get people out, when necessary.

Perhaps even their fortune-telling activities can be used to suggest to a susceptible, frightened populace that other futures are possible. No act of resistance is too small.

Perhaps most important of all, the Gypsies live on the margins, without property or privilege, and therefore have no vested interest in protecting the status quo. Neither pretence nor denial about what is happening serves a purpose; they have no illusions about the Germans' intentions. Only a fish gets caught twice by the same hook, they say.

Suzie plays her part in this process of preparation as the initial conduit, the message-bearer, the link. She's inconspicuous enough to meet the man in the white suit in churches or cafés without attracting undue attention; and she's trusted and known enough by the Gypsies to turn up wherever they are. She runs from one to the other with the determination and concentrated ferocity she once had as a child and has held in check ever since.

This ferocity finds its way into her love-making with Cesar, too. But one night, as they lie exhausted in long grass by the Seine looking at the columns of black smoke snaking into the sky in the distance – for the Germans are only forty kilometres away and are setting fire to the oil depots near Paris – Cesar asks Suzie who she is really fighting for and she cannot answer. She feels pushed away by him, because he seems to be telling her that in spite of everything she does not really belong with him or his people. But they both know that he is really pushing her away because at any moment they might be torn from each other, and so the greatest danger of all is to love too much because then the pain of separation will be unbearable when it comes.

And then, within a month of invading northern France, the Germans enter Paris at dawn, quietly, correctly and politely. Overnight, the deserted streets are full of soldiers, acting like tourists with their street maps and cameras, looking at the sights.

And that is how one of them, some days later, peering through the lens of the home-movie camera vibrating in his hand, sees two young women coming towards him across the bridge, one blonde, one dark, their hair glinting in the sunshine. The blonde smiles into his camera lens, flirtatiously, but the dark one turns her head away.

Lola has contacted Suzie, saying she has something important to tell her. But at first Lola talks only of herself as they walk the streets together under the cloudless blue sky. She confides that as a Russian she isn't entirely sure of her future in these new circumstances. Right now the Germans and the Russians are best friends, but it wasn't always so, and who knows? And she finds herself confiding, not just about the terrors she left behind in Stalin's Moscow, which somehow she had never mentioned before, but also about Dante's unfaithfulness now that she is his for the asking. About the nights she has spent alone in the echoing apartment as he goes God knows where, and men, you can never trust them once they've got what they want. And I thought I wanted him, only him, Suzie, but now I'm not so sure.

And then, when Suzie wishes her luck with all this and says she's sorry but she must go now, for she has things to do, Lola says in a small quick voice that she has learnt from something she has overheard at dinner from some of Dante's new German friends – and from their interest in Dante's free pronouncements about the people he knows, including Suzie herself – that Suzie should leave the country as soon as she can.

It's impossible, says Suzie, you know that.

And then, in the silence that falls between them: What about my friends?, asks Suzie, white with anger. Should they leave too? Should everyone leave?

I don't know about your friends, says Lola, but you are in danger. If your friends can get you to the coast, I think I can help you with the boat.

What boat?, asks Suzie.

The boat to America, says Lola, to America. Where you have always wanted to go, you told me often enough. And I will be on it too, she adds, looking away.

And the man in the white suit says, later, when Suzie manages to contact him, urgently, Yes, it's time for you to go, you've done what you can, but if you stay you'll do more harm than good.

But I'm the link, you know that, says Suzie, in a tight voice. Don't you need me anymore?

You've helped set up the network, he replies, kindly. And now it works. But if they get you, you will talk and everyone will be at risk.

But I won't talk, says Suzie, I know how to keep quiet, really I do.

You'll talk, he says, gently. Everyone does in the end.

And because they know it may be their last night together Cesar finally comes back to Suzie's little room. They stand on her narrow balcony and sway vertiginously in and out of the shadows, giddy with love and anguish, as they touch each other slowly, painfully, before Suzie falls on to her knees and clings to Cesar's legs saying, Don't leave me, never leave me, oh please don't go.

But he uncurls her fingers and carries her inside, into her bed, where they lie together, naked for the first time, and he weeps into her hair before saying, But it's you who is leaving, Suzie, you.

But I don't want to run any more, says Suzie. I've been running all my life and now I want to stay and fight.

But running is good, too, says Cesar. It's better to run and live than stay and die.

And then there are no words left and so they speak to each other with their bodies, making love in a mute and ecstatic communion.

When Cesar lies sleeping, at last, Suzie gets up and crosses the room and quietly empties the jar of sugar on to the table, and then takes her precious savings and lays them gently, lovingly, like an offering, beside his sleeping form. Because it's money, in the end, that can save a life.

Then she looks about her little room one last time, puts on her coat, takes the scrap of photo of her father from its hiding place, and slips away down the stairs to the escort waiting to take her on the next steps in the long, slow, interrupted journey she had begun so long ago.

She leaves Paris hidden in the back of a truck laden with sweet-smelling apples, is transferred at dawn to a trunk strapped to the underside of a Gypsy caravan, and finally, thirsty and exhausted, lies underneath the stinking, salty, heavy nets in a fishing boat at night.

And so it is that Suzie finds herself, eventually, in bright sunshine, side by side with Lola in a small boat, setting out across the choppy water in the harbour at Marseilles. And Lola, who had travelled south in relative comfort by train, has eyes only for the ocean liner anchored at the harbour's mouth. But Suzie is looking back through the white foaming spray at what she's leaving behind.

When they are aboard they find that the liner is packed with evacuees and anxious émigrés and Americans returning home, at last, from this terrible place they call Europe. Lola is ushered through the crowds to her cabin but Suzie is shown to crew quarters. For at night, in what under normal circumstances would be the first-class restaurant but now is also crowded with mattresses (for this may be the last boat out and they have squeezed in everyone they can), Suzie stands once again on a small stage, singing for her supper. For the first time she is dressed not in feathers or sequins but in her own simple clothes, singing songs that will help to keep the terrors of war at bay as they cross a U-boat-infested ocean.

Sitting at one of the tables, quietly watching her and listening, is Lola, dressed in velvet and diamante, leaning on the arm of an elderly American. Lola the lovely opportunist, Lola the survivor who's starting life all over once again. But when Suzie sings it's not just Lola but most of the tense and restless passengers who pause for a moment, forks suspended in mid-air, to listen to this dark-eyed girl, soothed and fortified by her lovely voice; a voice with a sob in the throat, a voice that somehow transforms the popular songs they thought they knew into something else, something resembling a prayer.

One night, after everyone else is tucked up in bed, Suzie and Lola meet on deck and Lola tells Suzie how the man she's met has promised to help her get to Hollywood, and isn't it strange how things turn out to be for the best; and Suzie, in reply, says that for her, on the contrary, it's ironic that now she is at last on her way to America she doesn't really want to go.

But your father, Suzie, that will be nice for you, to see him at last, says Lola. And Suzie pulls out the remains of the photo from her pocket and stares at it, saying, Yes. Perhaps.

And then later, when Suzie is alone on deck staring at the endless horizon and Lola is below, deep in the bowels of the ship, stretching her long beautiful limbs in the deserted Egyptian-style swimming pool, there is a sudden horrible thud, a short but endless silence and then a series of explosions that hurl Suzie into the air and into the dark water, where she surfaces, gasping for breath, to see the great ship on fire, sparks flying like mad fireworks all around her.

And Suzie is amongst the dazed, shivering survivors picked up from the wreckage of the torpedoed ship and bundled into blankets, who, some days later, will stand huddled on the deck of a small tramp steamer as it limps into New York City in the early hours of a grey and misty morning. And there, at the quayside, are a swarm of newsmen waiting with their cameras, darting about amongst the survivors, some of whom are said to be famous, and one of them asks her: Are you somebody?

But now she doesn't even have a photograph in her hand. All that remains of it is a sodden scrap of paper salvaged from her pocket with the blurred name of a man and an address in a small town in Russia just visible. And in her head she has the details of her father's clothing etched permanently into her memory from the hours she had spent gazing at his fading, shredded image.
   These clues are enough to lead her, with a little help from the immigration official at Ellis Island, to an organization of refugees from that part of Russia, and from there to a Jewish tailor who questions her closely about the cut of her father's coat, and its length, and was the collar like so, or so.

And when two and two have been put together she finds a man who knew a man who knew Mr Money (who had died a pauper along with his wife in a tenement fire) and who tells her he is sorry, but that the name on the scrap of paper belongs to a man who died as well. And what's more he died before he even left Russian soil, one of those who fell by the wayside just a few kilometres from his home town, victim of an angry peasant's misplaced rage. And in this terrible moment Suzie realizes that all is lost, and that her long journey has been pointless, pointless, and that she has been chasing nothing but a ghost since she was seven years old. And at first all she can do, after a moment of breathless silence, is to laugh.

But on the way out of the door she turns and says quietly: No, it's not possible, my father's voice could never die.

And the man says: Voice? This man was a photographer.

And so she finds the name written on the back of the photo was the name of the man behind the camera, not the man posing with such formality in front.

But of course, says the man, when Suzie describes how her father sang in the synagogue for all the town, and he tells how everyone remembers the tall thin cantor from the little town near Minsk whose voice thrilled them all when he first arrived in New York, but who famously wrote to the advice column in *The Forward*, the Yiddish newspaper, when he discovered that the shtetl where he had left his mother and his daughter had been burned to the ground and all its occupants perished, saying that he could no longer believe in a just God and therefore could no longer sing.

And how, after that, he had changed his name along with his personality and gone west, but perhaps if Suzie were to go to the nickelodeon where he had first found a job after he left the synagogue and renounced his faith she might find out where he ended up.

And the cashier at the nickelodeon on 7th Avenue, seeing Suzie's tired, despairing face, goes out of his way to help, saying, Cheer up, it could be worse. Your father, if you're really his daughter, is a millionaire. Because he worked like the devil you know, and if you work hard like that, and have a vision, you can succeed over here.

And so it is that Suzie finds herself in the bright white sunlight of Los Angeles, on the backlot of a film studio, looking about her at the men dressed as cowboys and the girls dressed as wedding cakes; at the replicas of saloon bars on the pioneer trail, and the painted sets of idealized streets in small-town America; at the automobiles and trailers and signs of money, money everywhere; and then she is staring at a photograph on a wall of a man they all call Big Daddy.

But this man isn't tall and thin any more, but thin and bent, and seems to be propped up by the girls in frothy white dresses that surround him.

Eventually Suzie manages to get the attention of one of the bronzed assistants dashing about carrying a clipboard who says, That's a new one, his daughter. What you girls will say to try to get a job.

But something in her eyes makes him relent and he leads her away and makes her sit in a chair in a busy corridor, eventually returning with a lady with an efficient smile who says, I think you had better see Big Daddy's lawyer.
I'd rather see my father, says Suzie.
If that's really what he is, says the smile, then you will see him. But he is not well, not well at all. In fact, he's in hospital. So let me tell you right now, if this is a sick joke I'll kill you.

But after an interrogation and a series of telephone calls made by the lawyer sitting behind a vast desk who is, it turns out, less intimidating than his secretary, Suzie finds herself at last following a nurse down a long, blindingly white hospital corridor.

And she walks and walks, taking the last steps on this long and broken journey, faltering only at the very end.
And then the door swings noiselessly open and Suzie sees him.
An emaciated man, grey in the face, he lies very still, wheezing, under the starched white covers in the immaculate, sterile room. The nurse bends down and whispers something in his ear and he slowly opens his eyes.

Suzie crosses the room and stands by the bed, the standing, healthy woman looking down at the sickly, dying man, until at last he asks her quietly, Can it really be you? I thought you were dead.

But she has been struck dumb, again. She cannot remember what a word is, or how to speak. Too much has happened, too many stories to ever tell.

It is only when he whispers, Fegele, my Fegele, my little bird, that the dam bursts and it comes flooding out of her in a torrent of wailing Yiddish, and then the nurse is there trying to drag her away, saying, Hush, you can't do that here, and Suzie says, Don't touch me, you can't make me leave, I won't go, I'll never leave him, ever, and you can't make me be quiet, no one can, don't you dare.

And then her father's hand slowly reaches for hers across the covers and she stops her wild protest for a moment and turns back to the old man lying in bed and sees a pleading, agitated, vulnerable look that takes her by surprise.

And then something turns in her and she finds herself reaching out to soothe the brow of this man whose stories she will probably never hear, and she starts to sing to him, softly, the lullabies he had once sung to her as a child. The fear and guilt and agitation in his face slowly melts and his eyes fill with tears.

And so it is that the man who had become a mogul, a myth-maker, a father of the American dream, closes the circle and becomes again the man who cried.

But as Suzie sings, and holds the dying body of her father, she stares into the distance as if she is seeing a ghost. For in this moment of remembering everything, she realizes not only what she has irrevocably lost, but also what it is that she has become. The ghost is herself, freed from her eternal and unrealizable longings at last.

The Man Who Cried

A young woman surfaces in a dark, tumultuous ocean while flames dance on the surface of the water all around her. She gasps, struggling for breath in the seething inferno of fire and water.

FRONT TITLES BEGIN — INTERCUT WITH . . .

A tall man – a cantor – singing joyfully at a village gathering, whilst his little daughter watches and listens, entranced by his voice and presence.

EXT. ROAD AND FOREST — DAY

The little girl cries out with joy as her father lifts her into the air and on to his shoulders. He carries her along a road through a forest.

TITLE: RUSSIA 1927

And then she is crawling through bracken and ferns and he is chasing her, playfully, calling her name.

FATHER

Fegele . . . Fegele.

But she runs away from her father along a track, deeper into the forest, laughing.

And then she hears a sound.
She crouches, and she watches intently.

It's a procession of horses and caravans; a group of Gypsies on the move.

EXT. VILLAGE — DAY

And now the man has lifted his daughter up again on to his shoulders and is carrying her home into their village. Small wooden houses, men and women going about their business; talking, fetching, carrying, working.

A rural shtetl – poor, busy; a community in which everyone knows everyone and everyone knows his or her place. Groups of men in long shabby dark coats and fur hats nod respectfully as their cantor passes them with his little girl.

And then, in the distance, a young man appears wearing a shiny blue suit and a racy hat, carrying a suitcase. He is handing out sweets and toys to the ragged children who appear and cluster around him, digging in his pockets for more.

Fegele's father puts her down and stands watching as the young man's mother throws her arms around him and wails with joy.

MOTHER OF MAN IN SUIT
(in Yiddish)
Yankele! My dear son! You came back from America!

And Fegele, clutching her father's hand, gazes up at his expression as he stares intently at the scene, preoccupied with something she does not yet understand.

INT. HOUSE — NIGHT

Fegele is lying in bed in the darkness. She sits up, eyes wide open, as she listens to the animated male voices in the kitchen. And occasionally, the soft, anxious, pleading voice of her grandmother, interjecting. And that word again: America.

VILLAGE MAN #1
(in Yiddish)
What is it really like in America?

VILLAGE MAN #2
(in Yiddish)
Can you earn enough to send for the family?

Fegele gets up and goes and stands in the doorway, barefoot, bewildered, watching the adults as they talk so urgently, questioning the young man in the shiny blue suit.

VILLAGE MAN #3
(in Yiddish)
Isn't it better to take them along?

MAN IN SUIT
(*in Yiddish*)

No. If you're alone you can save. In America, if you work hard anything is possible.

And then the group falls silent as one of them sees Fegele standing there.

Fegele's father turns and smiles at her, lovingly, then crosses the room, kisses her and takes her back to bed.

And then he is sitting on the edge of the bed, singing a lullaby, his special lullaby for her.

FATHER
(*singing in Yiddish*)

Close your eyes
And you shall go
To that sweet land
All dreamers know

Where milk and honey
Always flow
And Papa
Watches over you.

The little girl looks up adoringly at her father, held in the familiar comfort of his gaze and his lovely, soaring voice . . .

EXT. DOORWAY — DAY

Fegele is staring up at her father, wide-eyed, gripping on to his hand, as he stands outside their little house in his long dark coat, a meagre bundle of possessions at his side.

He strokes his little daughter's head, staring down helplessly at her, as tears start to form in his eyes.

Fegele's grandmother is trying to pull her away, coaxing her, cajoling, talking repetitively in a soothing voice.

GRANDMOTHER
(*in Yiddish*)

He will send for us. We'll have a new life, a better life in America. You must let him go. Let your father go.

She uncurls the child's fingers one by one from their furious grip, as she murmurs the words with all the conviction she can muster and then looks sadly at her son.

Goodbye, my son.

A group of men are standing waiting in the road, their bags tied to their backs. And amongst them, the man in the blue suit. The men are starting to mutter, anxiously.

And eventually, reluctantly, the tall man tears himself from his beloved daughter and walks away. He turns once more and they gaze silently at each other, a long, last, lingering look.

INT. KITCHEN – DUSK

Fegele and her grandmother are sitting at the table in the kitchen, silent and immobile, in front of two bowls of untouched cabbage soup, as darkness creeps into the room and folds itself around them.

Rain falls on to the house; hard, relentless rain. The grandmother gestures to her granddaughter.

GRANDMOTHER
(*in Yiddish*)

Eat.

6

But neither of them moves.

EXT. FOREST — DAY

Fegele is standing alone in the green light of some pine trees. She closes her eyes and breathes in the heady scent of pine, a look of loneliness and longing on her face.

EXT. FIELD — DUSK

Fegele is playing with a group of children in long grass.

They are playing a now familiar and endlessly repeatable game; some-one is leaving for America and someone is being left behind. It's serious work, this game, and they are intent in their play.

But then they are distracted by the sound of rumbling explosions and shouting voices.

> GRANDMOTHER
> (*in Yiddish*)
> Fegele! Fegele! Come quick!

INT. AND EXT. HOUSE — NIGHT

Shouts, cries, chaos. Wrinkled female hands reach up on to a shelf, take down a jar of sugar, and pour the sugar on to the table. Hidden in the sugar there are three gold coins.

> GRANDMOTHER
> (*in Yiddish*)
> God in heaven. Oh no, not again.

With trembling hands, the grandmother sews the coins into the lining of her granddaughter's coat, and then takes her by the hand and leads her outside into the dark and smoke and confusion.

And now a man is lifting Fegele up on to the top of a heavily laden cart behind two boys, as other villagers run past, clutching their belong-ings, shouting with fear.

> Wait! Wait!

She runs back into the house, reaches up and pulls down the framed photo of Fegele's father – formal, posed and already fading – and then rushes back out and thrusts the photo into the child's arms.

Keep this with you.

The man whips the horse and the cart lurches off, the little girl clutching the heavy framed photo to her body. Her grandmother waves a last goodbye.

EXT. VILLAGE – NIGHT

Fegele is sitting on top of the bundles of possessions on the back of the cart, staring about her as they drive through the remains of a burning village.

Crackling, hissing, black smoke.

And then some men lurch out of the swirling smoke and rush at the cart, dragging the man from the driving seat, hitting him and searching his pockets.

And then there is a gunshot. Fegele stares, soundlessly, at this terrible, meaningless act of violence.

One of the boys turns frantically and tugs at the hem of Fegele's coat. He wrenches out a gold coin and presses it into the hands of one of the men, who looks at the three frightened children and then whips the horse on. Fegele gazes back soundlessly as the cart lurches onwards.

She gazes at the man lying on the ground, at the running figures, and at the flames, shooting violently into the swallowing darkness as the remains of the village burns.

EXT. LANDSCAPE – DAY

One of the boys is uselessly trying to stuff a morsel of frozen grass into the horse's mouth as it lies dead by the side of the road in the middle of a vast, cold landscape.

And now Fegele and the two boys who are not yet men, but whose faces carry the weight of loss and responsibility, set off on foot along the endless road.

Fegele staggers under the weight of her photo and one of the boys rips the photo from its heavy wooden frame and throws the frame into the ditch.

INT. SHED AT PORT — DUSK

People are shouting and gesticulating in a stinking, crowded shed at the dockside. And in the midst of the mayhem are Fegele and the two boys, their clothes ragged and their shoes worn and filthy from their long, exhausting journey.

The boys are arguing with a man with gold teeth and a strange smile who holds a fist full of coupons and tickets. Finally, one of them rips out the second of the three gold coins from the hem of the child's coat and hands it over. The man with gold teeth bites the coin, nods, and puts it in his pocket. Then he pushes Fegele towards one exit as he gestures the boys towards another.

> FAT MAN
> (*in Russian*)
> Yes, America, America, that is where her boat is going as well, don't worry, trust me.

And the last that Fegele sees of the boys as she looks back through the surging crowds is a hand waving, and then they are gone.

INT. BOAT — NIGHT

Fegele lies in the darkness in the hold of a ship amongst the retching bodies of strangers, clutching the crumpled photograph of her father, staring sleeplessly about her as the ship rolls and heaves its way across the dark, endless sea.

EXT. QUAYSIDE (ENGLAND) — DAWN

A cold grey dawn. A long wall under a shelter at the docks. Notices everywhere that read BRITISH CUSTOMS, BRITISH IMMIGRATION — *for those that can read English.*

Fegele is one of a group of children, travelling alone, who are separated from the family groups and lined up against the wall to be inspected — for lice, for disease, for foreign and unnamable maladies of all kinds — by a woman from the British Red Cross.

And then an official carrying a clipboard is passing down the line giving each child the gift of a pronounceable name. He reads out the names in alphabetical order as a portly assistant with a florid face scribbles the names on to signs and hangs them round the children's necks. A starched lady in a Red Cross uniform stands behind each child and places her hands on their tiny shoulders as they are named.

OFFICIAL
Nancy. Olive. Pruscilla. Richard.

The official is standing behind him, running his finger down the list on his clipboard.
(*briskly*)
Susan.

ASSISTANT
(*kindly*)
Suzie, for a black-eyed little Susan, eh?

He looks down at Fegele, his large smiling face looming above hers.

She stares up at him, wide-eyed, stilled and silenced by exhaustion, by the terrors of abandonment, and now by bafflement at the incomprehensible sounds coming out from this strange man's mouth.

And then she's stretching out her hand to him. In her little palm is the last of the gold coins.

What's this, then?

SUZIE
(*whispering*)
America.

ASSISTANT
No. *England*, dear.

The assistant laughs a big hearty laugh and stuffs the coin back in her pocket.

EXT. ENGLISH HOUSE — DAY

The silent, starched lady in a Red Cross uniform leads the newly named Suzie up a garden path towards the front door of a house where a lady with red hair and a tight, anxious smile stands waiting, her ghostly husband hovering in the background.

INT. BATHROOM — NIGHT

The lady's smile never falters as the child's shabby coat is shaken violently and the gold coin the English customs official had refused falls from the pocket; and then, as the photograph, the only valued possession the child has, is taken from her.

RED-HAIRED LADY

Can I have that? Let me have that. Will you give it to me? Can't I have it?

At first the little girl clings to the photograph, wordlessly struggling, but finally, when she realizes that the bony adult fingers are infinitely stronger than hers, she yields with a quiet and terrible resignation and sees the photograph of her father pass into the hands of the red-haired lady's shadowy husband.

It's for her own good, mind, because it will only make her upset.

And then she is plunged into a bath — huge, steaming, white, antiseptic — and scrubbed clean, cleaner than clean.

There, that's better then, Suzie, isn't it? Nice and clean.

INT. BEDROOM — NIGHT

Suzie's new bedroom is cold and alien. A heavy dark wardrobe, a swirling floral carpet, long fussy curtains framing the high window. And, hanging above the bed like a warning, a tiny crucifix; Jesus, in agony, nailed to the cross.

Suzie sits perched on the edge of the bed in a candlewick dressing-gown, slippers dwarfing her tiny feet, and stares silently about her.

It's a silence that she wears like armour.

EXT. SCHOOL PLAYGROUND — DAY

In the school playground — a hard asphalt surface surrounded by a high brick wall — a group of children is surging around Suzie as she stands, silent and immobile. They are pointing and poking at her, curious and casually hostile, with the learned distrust of the foreigner.

> FIRST CHILD

Where are you from?

> SECOND CHILD

Where is she from?

> THIRD CHILD

She don't know.

> SECOND CHILD

She can't speak.

> THIRD CHILD

Maybe she don't speak English.

> FIRST CHILD

She's a Gypsy.

> SECOND CHILD

Gypsy!

> THIRD CHILD

Raggle-taggle Gypsy!

One of them pushes her. Then another.
But she doesn't resist. Just stares, uncomprehending at the jumble of sounds and noises all around her.

The clanging sound of a teacher's bell cuts through the babble and the children jostle into line.

INT. FRONT ROOM — NIGHT

The red-haired lady, her face shiny with cold cream, is running down the staircase towards the sound of breaking glass. She swings open the door of the front room, with its three-piece suite and its ornaments and framed photographs on the mantelpiece.

But now the framed photos of Mr and Mrs Red Hair at their wedding lie smashed on the floor and Suzie is sitting amongst the splinters and broken glass with a poker in her hand.

RED-HAIRED LADY

Stop it!

The lady picks up one of the smashed photos, looks at Suzie, and then slaps her, but Suzie doesn't cry, just stares up with dark eyes flaming. Her silence has become absolute.

EXT. PLAYGROUND AND ROAD — DAY

Suzie the silent outsider is watching from a distance as a group of girls play an elaborate skipping and clapping game in the morning break.

And then a boy shouts and the other children rush to the high iron gates and cluster there, peering out into the street.

CHILDREN

Gypsies! Come and look at the Gypsies!

Suzie follows them to the gates and looks out too at the horses, the caravans, the women in their bright clothes carrying baskets full of clothes pegs.

And when the school bell has called the other children to order Suzie is still staring through the gates at the figures as they disappear into the distance.

But now she has broken her silence and is singing, quietly, to herself in Yiddish, her native tongue.

SUZIE
(*singing in Yiddish*)

Close your eyes
And you shall go
To that sweet land
All dreamers know . . .

She sings in a small, beautiful, plaintive voice. A voice full of longing.

But someone is listening. The teacher on playground duty – a man in a worn tweed suit – has heard the dark, dumb girl singing.

He listens thoughtfully, attentively.

INT. ASSEMBLY HALL – DAY

And now the teacher is standing with Suzie in the middle of the vast, empty assembly hall. He is coaxing her to sing along with him. He sings a phrase at a time, and she tries to imitate him in her pure, lovely voice.

But this is a hymn, with English words, which he is trying to teach her, syllable by syllable, in a voice which has a trace of a Welsh accent.

TEACHER
All things bright and beautiful . . .

SUZIE
All, all . . .

TEACHER
Things.

SUZIE
Tings . . .

TEACHER
Things.

SUZIE
Tings . . .

TEACHER
Things . . . bright.

SUZIE
Brrr . . . brr . . .

TEACHER
Bright and beautiful. Bright.

Suzie wrestles with the English pronunciation.

SUZIE
(in Yiddish)
Ken nisht. Ken nisht. [I can't. I can't.]

The teacher immediately takes her little hand and hits it with his cane.

TEACHER
No. No more of that. You're in England now. So you speak
English, don't you?

*She looks up at him, confused, hurt, bewildered; hovering on the brink
of withdrawal, and silence.*

(kindly)
They didn't let me speak Welsh either. But it did me the
world of good . . . in the end.

He bends down and whispers to her conspiratorially.

You see, Suzie, you've got to learn to fit in.

INT. ASSEMBLY HALL — DAY

Suzie is standing on the platform in the school assembly hall, under an enormous wooden crucifix, singing, in English, to the school. A teacher in a black gown accompanies her on the tuneless upright piano.

The children, normally so restless, are still and silent as Suzie sings Purcell ('Dido's Lament' from Dido & Aeneas) *— in a small, pure, raw voice.*

                    SUZIE
                   (*singing*)
'When I am laid, am laid in earth,
May my wrongs create no trouble, no trouble in thy breast;
Remember me . . .'

The Welsh teacher in the tweed suit is standing proudly at the back of the hall, his arms folded across his chest. His eyes fill with tears.

The song continues . . .

INT. AUDITION ROOM — DAY

. . . but now Suzie is no longer a girl, though she is not yet quite a woman. She stands at one end of a wood-panelled audition room, singing the same song, in a voice that has matured but has retained much of its pure, direct quality.

                    SUZIE
                   (*singing*)
'. . . Remember me,
But ah! forget my fate . . .'

At the other end of the room, sitting behind a table, is a formidable-looking, middle-aged woman, with dark, dyed hair.

She watches and listens, frowning, twirling a pen in her fingers, as Suzie comes to the end of what is obviously now her audition piece.

WOMAN

Nice, dear, very nice. But I'm afraid a nice voice is not quite
enough. You see, our girls are famous on the continent for
their legs . . .

*Suzie hesitates momentarily, holding the hem of her skirt gingerly in
her hands. And then she boldly lifts it to reveal her legs, her head hanging slightly in embarrassment.*

*The formidable-looking woman sighs, puzzled, and slowly puts down
her pen.*

. . . and other things. Why *are* you here, actually, dear?

SUZIE

I want to go to America.

The woman smiles, knowingly.

WOMAN

Ah, I see. Another one. Well, I suppose 'Paree' is a step in the
right direction. And there's no harm in dreaming, dear, I like
a bit of ambition in my girls.

INT. FRONT ROOM — DAY

*Suzie is standing in the front room of the house that was never home,
saying goodbye to the lady with red hair and her silent, almost invisible
husband, standing beside her, a sad look of unspoken accusation on
both their faces.*

*The gold coin is handed to her. Suzie wraps it in a handkerchief and
puts it in her pocket. And then, at last, the photograph of her father is
returned to her. The photograph that was taken from her for her own
good and held in safe-keeping for this very day.*

INT. TRAIN — DAY

*Suzie staggers into the toilet of the train as it lurches and rattles on its
way to the English coast. At last she's alone and on her way.*

*She moves closer to the window, pulls the photograph out of her pocket,
and holds it up to the light, staring intently, devouring every detail. But*

as the train moves faster – swaying, lurching – the photograph in her hand becomes a jagged blur.

INT. ON STAGE (PARIS) – NIGHT

Suzie runs on to a stage in a small, seedy revue theatre. She is dressed in silver, one of the glittering group of girls famous on the continent for their legs, who pose in a tableau with their arms in the air . . .

INT. ROOM – DAY

Suzie flings open the shutters with a crash and light floods into a small room high amongst the rooftops in Paris.

Above the sink in a cupboard is a jar marked 'Sucre'. Suzie lifts it down and then takes the gold coin from her pocket and drops it into the sugar in the jar.

INT. ON STAGE – NIGHT

. . . and now Suzie is in another pose, stretching her arms towards a beautiful leggy blonde with a flashing smile.

The formidable lady with dark, dyed hair is watching proprietorially from the back of the theatre, looking at her girls past the blank, intoxi-

cated faces of the aging men in the audience as they silently, greedily, drink in the spectacle of youthful female flesh and energy ...

INT. ROOM — DAY

Suzie sits down on the bed, looks at her father's photo, now propped up on her bedside table, and then gazes around her new room with a little smile.

INT. ON STAGE — NIGHT

... and now the chorus of young women are in a line with their backs to the audience. The lights change to luscious pink, and the young women rotate their hips seductively.

EXT. PARK — DAY

Suzie is walking with her new friends from the revue along the gravel paths in a formal Parisian park. There's a jaunty swing in her stride.

Lola, the lovely dancer from Russia, voluble, voluptuous and full of blonde ambition, walks just ahead, leading the group.

Suzie looks at Lola admiringly. Lola turns back, hooks her arm through Suzie's and smiles at her.

LOLA

Do you speak French?

SUZIE

Not really.

LOLA

Well, I can teach you some words. A very important word that you must know is *amour* . . .

INT. SUZIE'S ROOM — DAY

The door opens to Suzie's little room and Lola walks in, gesturing expansively.

LOLA

So you live all by yourself, you poor little duck. Well, this is, you know, not too bad. Plenty of room.

She crosses the room and opens the windows.

(*murmuring to herself*)
In Moscow there would be three families in here.

And then she sees that Suzie has dropped some coins into the jar of sugar on the shelf above the sink.

LOLA

What are you doing?

SUZIE

I'm saving.

LOLA

What for?

SUZIE

To go to America.

Lola laughs.

LOLA

Suzie, you take my advice. Buy yourself a nice dress and you'll find a rich man who will take you there.

She looks at Suzie, expecting a smile, but Suzie is staring blankly at her with wide dark eyes. Lola shrugs and looks at her curiously.

And then Lola starts peering into cupboards, inspecting the room. Suzie quickly hides the photo of her father in a drawer whilst Lola's back is turned.

Lola leans back against the kitchen sink and smiles thoughtfully at Suzie.

I have a plan. I will help you find little extra jobs –

SUZIE

– what kind of jobs?

LOLA

Oh . . . cabaret at parties, Suzie . . . it's easy if you know the right people. And I will stay here with you. Yes? And we will share everything, everything. Then, maybe, we will have some money left in our pockets at the end of the week. It's a good idea, yes?

EXT. STREET MARKET – DUSK

Snow is falling. Suzie is standing in what seems to be a forest of pines. The trees cast a green light over her face in the frosty air. She closes her eyes and breathes in the scent of pine, a look of longing on her face.

But this is a street market filled to bursting with Christmas trees, and Lola is waiting just ahead. Suzie turns and follows Lola, and they link arms, laughing, as snow slowly drifts down around them.

EXT. ENTRANCE TO SUZIE'S BUILDING – DUSK

Suzie and Lola are carrying an enormous tree up the flight of stairs that lead to Suzie's building. They pass the concierge, who is looking out of her window.

The concierge raises an eyebrow and peers after them with her beady eyes as they stagger, laughing, up the staircase.

INT. ROOM – NIGHT

Suzie and Lola have crushed the tree into the tiny room where there are now two beds instead of one. Lola is decorating the tree. But then her attention turns inward, as she stands back from the tree to admire her handiwork.

> LOLA
> (*dreamily*)

Something is missing . . .

Suzie is sitting on the floor, a blanket wrapped around her shoulders.

> SUZIE

Like what?

> LOLA

The food . . . my friends . . . even the cold. This is *nothing*. Winter was *winter* in Moscow.

Lola sighs and then visibly appears to shake herself out of her reverie.

> (*brightly*)

But that's all finished with. Forward! Forward, we must always look forward. Isn't that true, Suzie?

She flops down on to a rug on the floor next to Suzie and starts idly thumbing through a magazine. But Suzie can see her sadness.

Suzie turns away and pulls out the photo of her father from its hiding place and shyly shows it to Lola.

> SUZIE

This is my father.

> LOLA

That's your father? Yes?

Lola glances at the faded image and then turns it over and stares at the lettering on the back. It is unmistakably written in Russian script, Cyrillic.

Abramovitch. But this is in Russian. Why didn't you tell me before?

Lola pores over the writing and finally deciphers the address written below the name.

> (*in Russian*)

It's near Minsk. So you're a Russian girl too! My God, you

keep a secret. From me, your friend! Is he alive?

But Lola is talking Russian in vain, because Suzie understands not a word. Lola stares at Suzie's blank expression.

(*in English*)
You don't understand Russian?

Lola looks down at the photo, at the clothes the tall thin man is wearing, and quietly repeats the man's name.

(*quietly*)
Abramovitch . . . Ah, but so, he was a Jew.

Suzie nods silently as Lola hands the photograph back to her.

EXT. CHÂTEAU – NIGHT

Glittering silver fireworks explode out of the darkness in the grounds of a château.

A white horse is the centre-piece of a tableau posed in front of the fireworks. A dark-skinned man (Cesar), holding a flaming torch, sits astride the horse.

Suzie stands to one side of the horse, dressed in sparkling gold, trem-

bling slightly in the cold and from the effort of holding her arms in the air in a pose. On the other side of the horse stands Lola, in a similar outfit and pose. The glamorous chattering guests cluster at the windows, laughing and pointing at the tableau. But as the fireworks splutter and fade the French hostess claps her hands and they turn away from the windows and move back into the warm, glowing, candlelit salon.

FRENCH HOSTESS
Silence, silence, everyone, please. Tonight we're lucky to have with us the guest star of Felix Perlman's new opera company. So, please welcome Dante Dominio, who has kindly agreed to sing something for us . . .

Two pale women seated side by side at a grand piano start to play an adaptation of an orchestral score ('Je Crois Entendre Encore' from The Pearl Fishers by Bizet).

Dante Dominio – tall, dark and elegant in immaculate evening dress – nods in acknowledgement of the rippling applause. And then he starts to sing.

As his glorious voice soars out above the glittering crowd, the chattering party-goers gradually fall silent. Felix Perlman, a slightly anxious-looking man dressed in a crumpled evening suit, watches their reaction with satisfaction.

Outside, Lola drops her pose and wanders across the gravel pathway. She stares in through the windows at the elegant jewelled women and at Dante, the focus of their gaze, and she slowly smiles. A smile that says, 'I want'.

But something more profound is stirring in Suzie as Dante's high, full, masculine voice floats out through the windows – a visceral sensation, a physical memory of her father's presence and vocal power – and she begins to tremble, uncontrollably. Cesar sits very still on his horse and watches the two women, the blonde with her gleaming smile peering in through the windows, and the dark-haired, trembling girl standing beside him.

He strokes the twitching, trembling neck of his horse, and then reaches out, instinctively, and puts a hand on Suzie's neck too, to quieten her, to soothe her trembling.

Suzie starts, violently, at his touch, and turns to look at him. Their eyes meet, briefly, but each recoils from the intensity of the other's gaze and they look away.

And now Dante has finished singing and Lola is manoeuvring her way through the crowd in the salon towards him. She leans towards him and whispers in his ear.

> LOLA
> (*whispering*)

You are *fantastic* . . .

Dante turns towards Lola and she flashes him a smile.

I just had to say that to you, that's all.

Dante laughs as he looks her up and down.

> DANTE
> (*laughing*)

Ah . . . the girl with the horse.

> LOLA
> (*laughing brightly*)

Oh, yes . . . But I don't usually do *that*.

> DANTE

Oh no?

> LOLA

Oh no. No. I'm a dancer, actually.

> DANTE

Ah . . . really?

> LOLA
> (*quickly*)

A *trained* dancer.

> DANTE

Aha. Where?

> LOLA

From Kirov.

Dante nods his head, smiling.

DANTE

So, you . . . ah . . . liked . . . it, then?

Lola smiles luxuriantly as she realizes that she has discovered how to hold his attention.

LOLA

Oh, yes . . . you are . . . you're *sublime*. I can't imagine, myself, how it must be to be on stage at the same time as you. Just somewhere in the background, listening to you . . . in the chorus, for example . . .

Dante smiles at Lola knowingly, and then, with an expression of largesse, snaps his fingers at Felix Perlman, who is hovering nearby.

DANTE

Felix!

FELIX

Yes?

DANTE

This . . . er . . . young Russian lady should come to your auditions.

Lola twinkles with gratitude and excitement. Felix forces a bright smile at Dante and is about to reply, when Lola continues.

LOLA

Oh, and I have a friend. She can sing.

Felix Perlman raises his eyebrows.

FELIX
(*ironically*)

Oh, is that so?

LOLA

She has a *lovely* voice.

Dante is gazing, admiringly, at Lola. He reaches out to touch her face.

DANTE

La bella bambola.

LOLA

. . . she's very talented.

FELIX

Do you sing too?

LOLA

No . . . well . . . I . . . a little, a little. But I dance.

INT. ON STAGE (OPERA) — NIGHT

The chaos of rehearsal.

Horses are stamping and tossing their heads in the confined space in the wings of the theatre as the orchestra crashes its way through a triumphal passage in the score ('Di Quella Pira' from Il Trovatore *by Verdi). The chorus of men and women in heavy soldiers' costumes are being hustled into position on stage as a backdrop shudders down behind them. Suzie and Lola are amongst them.*

Felix Perlman is watching from the auditorium, occasionally gesturing his directions.

Cesar is calmly coaxing his white horse on to the crowded stage as dry ice puffs out around them.

Dante Dominio is striding about, marking his positions on the stage, looking puzzled.

And then Felix Perlman is waving his arms and shouting as he makes his way on to the stage.

FELIX

Hold it! Hold it!

DANTE

Felix. You really want me to stand over there, huh? And not here?

Dante gestures to centre stage.

Felix shakes his head and points to the side of the stage.

FELIX

Over there, Dante. Here you block the entrance of the horse.

DANTE

The horse?

Dante stares at Felix, silently.

FELIX

It looks good, Dante.

DANTE

It? It looks good?
Felix, tell me. Is this opera or spectacle?

FELIX

I see no contradiction.

DANTE

Allora – I put it another way. Do you want the public to look
or to listen?

FELIX

Both, Dante, both. The eyes *and* the ears. It's opera for the
people. And the people need to be entertained.

*By now the chorus are listening attentively. Dante glances around at
them before replying.*

DANTE

I came to Paris to sing. Strangely, I believe the public are
coming to listen to me, not to look at scenery or horses.

*He smiles broadly, waiting for the laugh from the chorus, which comes
on cue. Felix freezes momentarily.*

But then what do I know, huh? I am just a foolish singer.

*Now that he has got everyone's attention Dante suddenly sings a
phrase full out, his magnificent voice filling the auditorium, and at once
the laughs in the chorus turn to sighs of admiration.*

Felix clasps his hands together appreciatively.

And then Dante Dominio saunters across the stage towards the wings.

Lola moves into his orbit and smiles.
It takes him a moment and then he recognizes her.

LOLA

Hello!

DANTE

Eccola! La bella bambola!

LOLA

Lola.

DANTE

Ah, Lola – *bellissima.* So now you are here with us, huh?

LOLA

Yes. Thank you very much.

Lola puts out a hand and lets it rest on his arm just a little too long, working her charms relentlessly, ruthlessly, now that her goal is clear.

DANTE

Bellissima.

He turns to go, smiling. Lola starts to follow him and gestures to Suzie to come with her.

Cesar is standing with his restless horse, calming and comforting him, apparently oblivious to all else. But he slowly turns his head and watches

Dante and the two young women as they disappear into the distance.

Suzie feels his gaze upon her back and looks round, instinctively, but Cesar has already looked away.

INT. CAR — NIGHT

Dante sits between the two women in the back of his chauffeur-driven car as they speed through the night along the shining boulevards.

Encouraged by Lola's admiring gaze and ready laughter Dante is expounding about music.

> DANTE
> Yes, it's a great, great aria. You see, Verdi understands that the voice can express the highest ideals for man. His search for strength and glory . . .

Dante glances towards Lola.

> (*smiling*)
> . . . and beauty.

Lola tosses her head flirtatiously and then, laughingly and deliberately, turns away and looks out of the window.

> (*murmuring*)
> Madonna.

INT. BAR — NIGHT

Dante, Lola and Suzie sit at a bar on high stools.

Lola is not wavering in her relentless, appreciative attention.

> LOLA
> But what is it like to be a star, to have everyone looking at you all the time?

Dante shrugs modestly.

> DANTE
> I was not always where I am now.

> LOLA
> Really?

DANTE

Oh no. When I was a child we had nothing. Nothing!

LOLA
(*murmuring*)

But that is incredible.

DANTE

We were immigrants. *Allora*. From the South of Italy to the North. Brrr!

Dante shivers melodramatically. Lola laughs and clucks sympathetically.

LOLA

It was cold?

DANTE

It's the people. They look down on you if you come from the South.

LOLA

How terrible.

DANTE

And because we were poor, we all lived in one little room. The whole family.

LOLA

No! The whole family?

DANTE
(*in Italian*)

Everyone. The whole family.

LOLA

That must have been *so* difficult for you.

Suzie watches and listens as Lola laughs and flatters her way ever closer to the man she now so obviously wants and must have.

INT. CAR — NIGHT

And now they are back in the car.

But this time Lola is sitting in the middle, between Suzie and Dante.

Suzie gradually shrinks into her corner as Lola edges ever closer to Dante, teasing him with her perfumed presence.

STREET EXT. CAR — NIGHT

Suzie is standing in the road outside her building, waiting for Lola, who is still sitting next to Dante. Dante is holding Lola's hand and whispering to her, smiling.

> DANTE
>
> Come on.

But she pulls away from him, shaking her head.

> LOLA
>
> No!

And then she flashes him a radiant, flirtatious smile, as she slowly and deliberately leaves the car.

INT. ROOM — NIGHT

Suzie is lying in her narrow bed watching whilst Lola sits on the other bed, gazing at herself in a mirror.

> LOLA
>
> Did you see how he looked at me?
> You see, Suzie, there are rules of how you get your man.

> SUZIE
>
> Rules? What rules?

> LOLA
>
> Well, first, you must play hard to get. If it is too easy, he loses interest. He must feel that he is a hunter and you are a beautiful wild animal he is hunting. It's a primitive instinct, you see.

Suzie lies and stares at Lola, silently.

> And, second, if you want to make a man want you and *only* you, then you must smile and you must listen, always listen.

He needs attention. Men, you see, they are very, very fragile.

Lola pauses for a moment and examines her reflection thoughtfully.

And, third, you must look good. Very good. Actually that's probably the most important thing of all. You know, without my looks, I would never have got out of Russia. Never.

And then her confident, conspiratorial tone wavers just slightly, and she turns towards Suzie questioningly.

Can you tell me something frankly, Suzie? Do you think I should get my hair bleached some more or should I leave it like this?

INT. ON STAGE — NIGHT

It's the first night of the opera. Everything has somehow come together.

Suzie and Lola are amongst the chorus, dressed as soldiers. But their attention is focused on Dante as his voice soars out above the chorus, above the crashing chords at the end of his aria.

Thunderous applause from a full house.

Felix stands watching in the shadows at the back of the auditorium as Dante drinks in the applause ecstatically, his arms extended to the people, his public.

EXT. BOAT ON RIVER SEINE — NIGHT

The cast and management of the opera are partying on a boat on the river Seine. Some are drunk and others high on theatrical camaraderie as the night comes to an end. In the centre of it all is Dante with the indefatigable Lola gazing adoringly at him. Felix Perlman is sitting nearby. A diminutive English reporter is interviewing Dante, accompanied by a photographer.

ENGLISH REPORTER
So what do you think explains the rise of Fascism in your country?

DANTE
An artist must be above politics. Don't you agree, Felix?

FELIX

So they say.

DANTE

But . . . you know . . . there has been chaos and confusion in my country. Mussolini believes in order and organization. He understands that the Italian people must gain back their self-respect.

ENGLISH REPORTER
(*smiling*)

By putting on black shirts and marching up and down at one of those rallies?

Dante stares down at him, uncertain if he is being mocked. But then he laughs and slaps the reporter's face playfully.

DANTE

You intellectuals! For the working man the rallies are about dignity and strength. The lighting, the music, the choreography . . . it creates an atmosphere . . . *magnifico*!

FELIX
(*ironically*)

Mussolini certainly has a great sense of theatre.

DANTE

Certo, huh? And everything he does, is . . . is *big*.

Suzie moves away from the giggling, appreciative group surrounding Dante and stands alone at the back of the boat, gazing out at the river.

You could learn something, Felix. He really knows how to reach his public, huh?

Suzie is watching a wedding party crossing the bridge. One of the women in the procession is throwing rose petals over the bride and groom. Suzie watches as the petals drift down through the night air on to the dark river water.

INT. BACKSTAGE CORRIDOR AND OFFICE — NIGHT

It's pay day.

37

A queue has formed in the corridor where Felix Perlman sits behind a desk, handing out money to the chorus and stagehands.

Cesar has just been paid and is painstakingly counting his wages, speaking in Romany.

And then Dante appears and sweeps to the head of the queue. Felix discreetly hands him an envelope.

DANTE
Felix! Thank you very much.

Then Dante notices that Cesar is signing in the ledger, slowly and carefully, with an 'X'. When Dante sees this mark of illiteracy, he makes grunting sounds and ape movements to amuse the chorus girls, who, as usual, are watching his every move.

Lola giggles but Suzie stares at Dante coldly.
Lola looks at Suzie, puzzled.

LOLA
(*whispering*)
They're just Gypsies.

DANTE
Let's go, *ragazze. Avanti.*

Dante reaches out impatiently to the two women.

But Suzie shakes her head.
A silent no.

Dante is startled by Suzie's refusal. A shadow of disbelief passes momentarily over his face. Lola laughs, brittle, and takes Dante's arm. He shrugs, bemused, and they saunter off.

And then Cesar and Suzie's eyes meet, and, for the first time, neither of them looks away. Cesar stares at her, as if to say he's been through this before; it's nothing new, and he won't give Dante or anyone else the power to hurt him.

Suzie holds his gaze, listening to this silent message. An alliance has been formed.

INT. CAFÉ — NIGHT

Cesar ushers Suzie into a noisy, shabby, crowded café.

A group of Gypsy musicians are playing to the raucous, chattering crowd.

They sit at a table, Cesar occasionally glancing at Suzie's face as she looks about her, listening to the fast, ecstatic music ('Bangi Khelimos') and watching a man who is dancing.

Suzie is entranced by the vitality, the noise, and is flushed with energy from having refused Dante and relinquished a role in his entourage.

The man who has been dancing approaches the table, extends a hand to Suzie and looks questioningly at Cesar. Cesar nods his permission. The man pulls Suzie to her feet. She is shy, at first, and reluctant, but then it's as if a firework has gone off inside her and she dances with a spirited ferocity that takes Cesar by surprise.

As she dances, he gazes at her with curiosity and desire.

INT. ROOM — NIGHT

Lola is watching Dante as he moves slowly around the room she shares with Suzie. She looks a little embarrassed as he touches the rickety table and the narrow beds; as he runs his white, smooth hands over the backs of the chairs and along the edge of the stone sink.

He gestures at one of the beds, which has a silky dressing-gown draped on the pillow.

DANTE
So you sleep here? And your friend sleeps over there?

He gestures at the other bed.

LOLA
(*in Russian*)

Yes.

But Dante is not looking at her. He is lost in a haze of dreamy sensuousness and regret as he murmurs a litany of remembrance.

DANTE
This is how it was for me. Yes, this is how it was. My mother and the baby in one bed, and my brothers and me in the other, end to end.

And now he is sitting on Lola's bed, gazing at her as she crosses the room slowly towards him.

The sacrifices my mother made for me . . .

He pulls Lola towards him, suddenly soft, tender and seductive.

Lola sinks on to his lap, relieved, with a small triumphant smile. Their lips are about to meet when Dante suddenly pauses, preoccupied. His brow furrows.

But why? Why did your little friend refuse my invitation?

But Lola does not answer. She moves in closer. They kiss.

EXT. STREETS — NIGHT

Suzie and Cesar are walking, silently, side by side, Cesar leading his beloved white horse behind them. The only sound is the horse's hooves, echoing in the empty streets.

EXT. SUZIE'S BUILDING — NIGHT

As they reach the entrance to Suzie's building she turns to face Cesar, shyly, expectantly.

They look into each other's eyes. And then he makes a move towards her, as if to touch her face, but she startles and backs away.

Cesar stands very still, staring down at her, hovering on the brink of sexual aggression. But then he makes a gesture of acceptance and backs away, smiling.

And then, still smiling, he leaps on to his horse and gives Suzie a brief display of subtle horsemanship, guiding his horse with minute signals to bow down to her.

She watches, quietly, flushed with pleasure.

And then, like an arrow, he's off, cantering flamboyantly into the distance.

INT. ROOM — NIGHT

Suzie runs up the stairs, excited, confused, alive.

But then she stops in her tracks on the landing outside her door when she hears the unmistakable sounds of Dante and Lola making love inside.

INT. ROOM — NIGHT

And now Suzie is lying in her bed, paralysed by shame and humiliation, an unwilling witness to Lola and Dante's love-making in the narrow bed on the other side of their tiny room.

But then Dante's groans and sighs of pleasure become whimpers and Suzie hears how Dante softly weeps when he has come and lies, still, vulnerable and open in Lola's arms.

Suzie lies staring into the darkness, helpless and excluded, as Lola comforts Dante, holding him in her arms and stroking him as if he were a little boy.

EXT. ENTRANCE — DAY

Suzie is walking down the stairs, crossing the yard, looking drawn, pale and tired after her sleepless night.

The concierge, Madame Goldstein, who is sweeping the yard, peers out at her with an irritable expression.

> MADAME GOLDSTEIN
> (*grumpily*)
> It's too big for you, the room? Perhaps soon there will be not two, not three, but four occupants in residence?

And then she shakes her head and exclaims in Yiddish.

> (*in Yiddish*)
> God in heaven!

Suzie freezes as something in her recognizes this forgotten language, and she stares at Madame Goldstein.

SUZIE

Would you say that again, Madame Goldstein?

Madame Goldstein repeats it willingly, and more.

MADAME GOLDSTEIN
(*in Yiddish*)

God in heaven, how many people can fit in such a room?

But it's no use, because it's only the first exclamation that Suzie remembers, imprinted dimly in her memory in her grandmother's panicking voice. Madame Goldstein stares at Suzie, with a slow look of recognition.

(*in English*)

So now I understand why you didn't seem like the other English girls.

INT. CONCIERGE'S ROOM — DAY

And now Suzie is sitting in the concierge's room, with its heavy East European furniture and piles of books, and Madame Goldstein is solicitously feeding her little cakes.

MADAME GOLDSTEIN

Eat.

SUZIE

Thank you.

And then Madame Goldstein puts a record on the gramophone.

She peers at Suzie, who is staring at her, wide-eyed with memory and longing, as she listens to the familiar music filling the room.

INT. DRESSING-ROOM — NIGHT

Lola is surrounded by other women in the chorus who are cooing admiringly over a necklace Dante has given her. Lola is flushed, triumphant; her eyes glittering.

LOLA

Isn't it gorgeous?

One of the women gestures at a twinkling dress.

CHORUS WOMAN

Did he buy that too?

LOLA

Yes! And you would not believe some of the restaurants he
has taken me to. Oh, my God! I've never seen such luxury!

*Lola stares at herself admiringly in the mirror. She can hardly contain
her excitement. Suzie looks regretfully at Lola, the friend she seems to
have lost. And then looks at her own reflection in the dressing-room
mirror; unglamorous, un-made-up, in her plain, simple frock, as Lola's
voice chatters on in the background.*

It's a beauty this one. Oh! Don't touch it! Your hands are
dirty . . . It fits me like a glove. He knows my size . . . I can't
tell you how he knows, but he knows it!

And then something changes in Suzie's face. A decision.

EXT. STREETS — NIGHT

*Cesar and the two other horsemen are trotting along a wide empty
boulevard in the centre of Paris. Suzie is riding a bicycle, pedalling
after them at a discreet distance.*

*The horsemen stop. Cesar inclines his head slightly and listens. He
smiles as he becomes aware of Suzie's presence. And then Cesar and
his companions set off at a gallop across the vast Place de la Concorde, past the glittering fountains, and Suzie is pedalling furiously in
pursuit.*

*Bridges, dark streets, occasional glimpses of the river, all melt into a
blur as she tries not to lose sight of the horses' swishing tails and the
three men's backviews, relaxed and upright as they gallop home.*

*And then the three men rise and stand on their saddles, urging their
horses on, faster and faster.*

EXT. WASTELAND — NIGHT

*And now Suzie is leaning her bicycle against a fence in the shadows
overlooking a stretch of wasteland, surrounded by semi-derelict build-
ings, overgrown railway tracks and abandoned railway carriages.*

There, in the distance, is a collection of caravans and tents, surround-ed by heaps of scrap, rusting wheels, old carts, the hulks of abandoned cars. It's a scene of poverty and improvisation. And life.

Men and women are busy at their tasks; stoking the glowing fires, feed-ing the horses in an enclosure. Tiny chattering children are running about everywhere. Dogs are barking.

Suzie peers through the railings, watching it all.

But then she becomes aware that some children are wheeling away her bicycle.

She runs after them, shouting, but they won't let go of the bicycle, and she starts to panic.

SUZIE

Children! Stop! Please!

As she chases them she is lead, irrevocably, into the heart of the camp. The Gypsies fall silent as they turn and stare at the arrival of the stranger. But then Cesar emerges from behind his white horse and smiles.

EXT. GYPSY ENCAMPMENT — NIGHT

A group of women lead Suzie through the camp, talking and gesticulat-ing. They lead her under a canvas awning where they pour water over her hands in a ritual act of ablution and welcome.

EXT. GYPSY ENCAMPMENT — NIGHT

A long table has been set up and is covered with food: bread, meat, tomatoes.
Suzie is seated at the end of the table, surrounded by the men as they eat and talk and laugh. The women serve food or hover at a distance. Children clamber everywhere.

Suzie gradually eases into the warmth and chaos. A dreamy look comes into her eyes, a long-forgotten familiarity with the feeling of being contained by a poor but vibrant community.

Cesar sits next to her. She watches as a child climbs on to his lap.

SUZIE

Is she yours?

CESAR

All the children here are mine.

He smiles at Suzie's startled expression.

And all the older ones are my parents. We are family. We are one.

Suzie looks at Cesar with dark eyes full of longing and, perhaps, even of envy. And then of confusion. Has he answered her question or not?

And then a man stands up and starts to sing at the other end of the table ('Baladele Revoluteii'). Some of the others pick up their instruments and play with him. One by one the other old men sing in turn, each addressing their guest, the stranger at the table.

When the song is over the Gypsies turn to Suzie, expectantly. One of them opens his mouth and mimes for her, Cesar's friend, the guest from the opera, an invitation to sing, to sing for them.

Suzie turns to stone.
She looks at Cesar imploringly.

But he just looks at her, implacably, and smiles.

And so, hesitantly, shyly, she starts to sing; the song she had once sung to the school as a child, and then at her audition ('Dido's Lament').

SUZIE

(*singing*)

'When I am laid, am laid in earth . . .'

The Gypsies listen politely.

And then a man picks up his accordion and starts to accompany her. As Suzie continues singing, the rhythm and harmonies subtly change, as one by one the others join in with their instruments.

And gradually a different sound creeps into Suzie's pure soprano voice. The hint of a sob in the throat. The hint of a voice from a tradition of ecstatic prayer; languid, sensual, intense.

(singing)
'Remember me, remember me . . .'

Cesar watches and listens.

INT. STAIRCASE — NIGHT

Suzie leaves her bicycle in the entrance hall and is slowly climbing the steep stairs to her room when she hears Lola's tinkling laugh and Dante's murmuring voice.

Something stops her in her tracks, something instinctively makes her wait unheard in the shadows, as she realizes that Dante is looking at the photograph of her father.

DANTE
Who is in the photo?

LOLA
Dante, why are you looking at that? It's just a photo of her father.

DANTE
Ah, so the little English girl has a secret. She's not what she seems, huh?

Suzie turns and tiptoes away down the stairs, shivering.

INT. CONCIERGE'S ROOM — NIGHT

Suzie knocks on the concierge's door and peers in through the window. Madame Goldstein is in the middle of listening to a broadcast on her wireless and gestures for Suzie to come in.

MADAME GOLDSTEIN
It has happened. My God, it has happened, like I knew it would.

SUZIE
What has happened?

Madame Goldstein gestures for Suzie to sit down.

48

MADAME GOLDSTEIN

I got out in time but . . . my father, he said he was too old to walk a step . . .

Suzie leans forward, staring at Madame Goldstein.

SUZIE

Madame Goldstein, what has happened?

MADAME GOLDSTEIN

Germany has invaded Poland. Now England and France must declare war on Germany. They can't just sit back and watch the Nazis grab any country they want.

Madame Goldstein walks to her stove where she starts to absently ladle some hot soup into a bowl. And then she turns towards Suzie, aware of her silence.

But here they will never come, child. It's the land in the East they want.

Madame Goldstein carries the bowl of soup to the table, puts it down in front of Suzie, who is staring up at her, wide-eyed, and then places a hand gently under her chin.

(*reassuringly*)

Don't worry, we're safe here, in Paris. After all, this is the country where they wrote the Declaration of the Rights of Man. *Liberté, egalité, fraternité* . . .

They stare at each other, silently. And then Madame Goldstein gestures at the untouched bowl of soup.

Eat.

INT. DRESSING-ROOM – NIGHT

A group of women in the chorus are crowded round a dressing-table, peering at a newspaper. Dante's voice can be heard singing an aria on stage in the distance ('E Lucevan le Stelle' from Tosca *by Puccini).*

FIRST WOMAN

Why should we care what Germany does in Poland?

SECOND WOMAN

I agree. They're always fighting about something over there.

THIRD WOMAN
(*quoting from the paper*)

Like it says here, who wants to die for Danzig? Where the hell *is* Danzig, anyway?

Lola and Suzie are sitting nearby quietly, looking at themselves in their dressing-table mirrors and listening to the others chatter.

LOLA
(*muttering*)

On the Baltic sea. Left of Russia.

The women glance in her direction and then continue in a whisper.

FIRST WOMAN

And why should we care what Germany does at home, come to that? They must have their reasons.

SECOND WOMAN

I agree. It's none of our business.

FOURTH WOMAN

But do you think they're right? Do you think the Jews are really controlling everything?

There's a pause in the conversation. Lola and Suzie both freeze momentarily.

FIRST WOMAN

Who do you think is controlling the money here? Right here in the theatre? I don't think Monsieur Perlman is a Catholic.

She shrugs, and the others laugh, anxiously.

And Suzie keeps brushing her hair, her eyes full and dark, barely able to believe what she is hearing.

INT. ON STAGE — NIGHT

And now Suzie is standing at the back of the stage, listening intently, as Dante concludes his aria, his magnificent voice sobbing with intensity and emotion.

But then he turns, confused, as laughter ripples through the auditorium. The horse standing on the stage, its bridle held by Cesar, has lifted its tail and shat.

Cesar smiles to himself.

A look of rage and humiliation passes over Dante's face.

INT. BACKSTAGE — NIGHT

Dante is being soothed by Felix Perlman as he paces furiously back and forth.

> DANTE
>
> That's it. Finished. *Finito. Che cazzo!* No more horses. No more *shit* on the stage. No more *dirt* in the theatre.

> FELIX
> (*soothingly*)
>
> Dante, please, don't take it personally. The horse was not making a comment on your performance.

> DANTE
>
> Be careful, Felix. You need me for the success of your little project.

FELIX

I think it would be more accurate to say that we need each other, Dante.

DANTE
(*icily*)

Non lo so. The people come. They pay. I sing. They applaud. You are just the ticket-taker. The man in the middle.

FELIX

Thank you, Dante – I take that as a compliment.

DANTE
(*icily*)

I could be singing in any theatre in Europe –

FELIX

Yes . . .

DANTE

– but I agreed to sing in yours. However, I do not recall a clause in my contract saying I was joining a circus. A Gypsy circus. *Va fanculo!*

Dante gestures towards Cesar, who is standing to one side with the offending horse, adjusting the saddle, stroking its neck, apparently unconcerned, as he waits for the storm to pass.

Suzie is watching Cesar, waiting for a reaction, but there is none. And Felix, too, is eloquent in his silence.

Now Dante is addressing Cesar directly.

You Gypsies should go back where you belong. You have no place in the world of the opera. You understand me?

Cesar kneels quietly, clearing up the offending horse droppings, ignoring Dante, implacable in the face of his fury.

You. I talk to you.

And then something snaps in Suzie and she speaks in a small, angry voice.

SUZIE

His name is Cesar.

Cesar glances up at the mention of his name, a small frown on his face. Dante wheels round to look at Suzie, startled.

This is a side of Suzie that has not been visible before. Suzie the defender.

DANTE

Alora, alora. She speaks, *la brunetta*, huh?

Dante turns to Lola, who is hovering nearby, and addresses her in a tone of high sarcasm.

She speaks to them, but not to *me*.

Suzie looks at Dante's puzzled, hostile face. And at Lola, anxious, appeasing, on the verge of disowning her friend, tension and conflict etched in her beautiful face.

SUZIE

Perhaps I do. And why not?

DANTE
(*in a stage whisper*)

They are dirty.

He wrinkles his nose with disgust.

SUZIE

How would you be if you lived on the road?

And now Cesar stares angrily at the young woman who wounds his pride in her attempt to defend him.

DANTE

Ah, well, but I don't. I live in an apartment with two bathrooms and beautiful furniture which I pay for with money I have earned. And why do they live like that? Because they are dirty, lazy thieves. Because they don't want to work, to make something of themselves.

SUZIE

They live on the road because their homes were taken away. They have nowhere else to go.

Dante stares after Suzie as she walks off the stage. Lola looks down. She doesn't want to see what she is seeing.

DANTE
(*whispering*)
Alora, Lola. Your little friend has become a Gypsy lover.

Dante turns on his heel and strides off the stage. Lola clatters anxiously after him.

EXT. YARD — NIGHT

Suzie steps into the yard outside the theatre.

And there is Cesar, waiting for her, standing silently by his horse. He stares at her, mute, burning with a quiet fury. And then he speaks, in a low, angry voice.

CESAR
I don't need you to fight for me. I don't need any woman to fight for me.

SUZIE
I was fighting for myself.

CESAR
And you say I am dirty? You, who are one of them; the *gadje*, the unclean?

SUZIE
No, no. I said . . .

Suzie stumbles, suddenly incoherent. They stare at each other, faces and eyes flaming.

Why are you accusing *me*? I am not one of *them*.

Cesar walks towards her, slowly, questioningly.

CESAR
Then what are you?

EXT. WASTELAND — NIGHT

And now Cesar is galloping in a circle around Suzie as she sits in a

battered armchair on a stretch of wasteland in the darkness near a
blazing open fire. He traces a figure-of-eight on the ground with Suzie
at the centre of one circle, and another fire at the centre of the other.

The only sounds are the sound of the horse's hooves pounding into the
dirt and the horse's breath and the crackling fire.

And now Cesar is pulling Suzie's head back, gently but forcefully, as if
to say, and I can control you too, I am as much of a man as him and
more. And you are a woman, like any other woman.

But something in Suzie's direct gaze disarms him.

Cesar reaches out and touches Suzie's lips, gently, with his fingertips.

And then finally, on this desolate wasteland, near an abandoned, rusting car, the embers of the fire glowing in the distance, they become
lovers. And the expression on Suzie's face shows that this is the first
time for her, but that despite the pain, she feels, at least for these timeless
hungry moments, that she can let go at last.

And Cesar is shocked and flattered; and he strokes her, tenderly, and
speaks to her in Romany in the soft, cooing voice he usually reserves for
his beloved horses.

> CESAR
> (in Romany)
> Lashoríye . . . shukaríye . . . ash, ash. [Fine little one, beautiful
> little one, be still, be still.]

INT. ROOM — DAY

Suzie is splashing her face with water, slowly and sensuously, standing
by the window, while Lola is taking her collection of sparkly gowns,
shoes and underwear and is packing them into a suitcase laid on her
bed.

> LOLA
> No more boring money problems. I can't believe it! . . . He's
> a very kind man, Suzie.

Lola turns to Suzie with a bright, forced smile. Suzie is watching her
calmly.

SUZIE
(*quietly*)

I thought you said you would never move in with a man
unless you were married. I thought that was one of your
rules.

*Lola scrutinizes Suzie as she dries her naked, glowing face with a towel
and looks at Lola with an open, direct gaze.*

*Lola pats her own hair, which suddenly looks a little brassy, and
smoothes down her dress.*

LOLA
(*in a hollow voice*)

Who says we won't get married? He adores me. And why do
you criticize me all the time? Don't you want me to be
happy? Don't you want me to look nice and eat well? Why do
you accuse, always accuse?

SUZIE

But I don't. I haven't said a word.

Lola snaps her suitcase shut and stares coldly at Suzie.

LOLA

No. You and your kind never do.

INT. DANTE'S APARTMENT — DAY

*The sound of Dante's full, voluptuous voice singing an aria full of love
and longing ('Je Crois Entendre Encore'), as Lola, wearing a pink
silky dressing-gown, twirls through Dante's grand apartment, laughing
with pleasure. She can hardly believe her luck, and she's letting it show.*

*Dante stands to one side, leaning against a door frame, his arms folded,
watching her proprietorially and smiling as she wafts excitedly towards
him, her arms outstretched, gesturing extravagantly.*

*But he can't help twitching as she falls theatrically into his arms and
accidently knocks over an ornament. Something that cost serious
money. He reaches out to steady it . . .*

57

INT. DANTE'S APARTMENT — NIGHT

And then Dante is on top of Lola, thrusting into her, as she lies on the ivory satin sheets in his large bed. Beside the bed are his velvet slippers, neatly placed; and, on the dresser, in front of the gleaming mirror and crystal bottles of eau-de-cologne, his silver hairbrushes in neat rows.

The sound of his singing voice continues over as Dante climaxes and Lola holds him in her arms, expectantly, watchful and waiting, but he turns his head away and lies silent and inert beside her.

INT. ROOM — NIGHT

Suzie sits up, suddenly, with a shout, woken by the sound of screams and breaking glass.

She gets out of bed, crosses the room and opens the doors on to her balcony. The stars are twinkling in a velvety night sky over the peaceful sleeping rooftops of Paris.

INT. DANTE'S APARTMENT — DAY

Lola is lying in a bathtub flicking through a pile of magazines, lonely and bored. She settles back into the deep bath water with a sigh as Dante's voice continues singing . . .

INT. ON STAGE — NIGHT

... *the aria ('Je Crois Entendre Encore') on stage whilst Felix Perlman sits listening quietly in the wings. Dante spreads his arms wide to his public. The music continues over . . .*

INT. CINEMA — NIGHT

... *Lola in a cinema watching a black-and-white film of a water-ballet. Some women dive in unison into a glittering pool, and form themselves into a floating mandala.*

Lola looks pensive, absorbed; lost in the watery images washing over her. And then her gaze turns inwards.

The image on the screen becomes Lola herself, transformed into a glamorous bathing belle, swimming in turquoise shimmering water, her red lips parted in a radiant smile. She starts to twist and turn luxuriantly, swimming on her back and then her front, gracious as a gleaming silver fish, and smiling, always smiling . . .

INT. UNDER THE STAGE — NIGHT

... *Dante continues to sing his aria, whilst under the stage, in the dust and shadows, leaning against a pillar, Suzie and Cesar are making love, passionately. The music continues over . . .*

INT. RESTAURANT — NIGHT

... *Dante holding forth to a circle of friends and admirers. The admirers are listening appreciatively and laughing, especially the women.*

Lola is sitting opposite him. She smiles, bravely, and tries to flirt with the other men at the table, but her heart isn't in it. She's too busy watching where Dante is looking; the little signals that pass between him and the other more aristocratic French women; their pale, bejewelled hands resting gently on his arm.

Lola smiles at Dante coquettishly but he looks at her coldly and turns away. Her smile fades in dawning realization as his aria comes to an end.

EXT. STREET — DAWN

Suzie is wheeling her bicycle slowly home in the early light of day, looking slightly sleepy and dishevelled, when she realizes something is wrong. There are two shiny black vans parked at the end of her street. Bewildered, frightened faces are peering out. And a babble of voices — Czech, Hungarian, Yiddish . . .

And then, suddenly, there is Madame Goldstein being frog-marched out of the building by two men and bundled into the back of the waiting van.

Suzie drops her bike and rushes up to the van as they slam the doors shut.

The van pulls away and Suzie runs after it, staring helplessly at Madame Goldstein's face peering out piteously from the window.

INT. ROOM — DAY

Suzie lurches into her room, crying. She picks up the photograph of her father and starts talking through her tears to the remote, fading image.

                              SUZIE
    What shall we do? . . . I don't know what to do.

But the photograph remains mute and impenetrable.

EXT. PLACE DE LA CONCORDE — DAY

Suzie is pushing her bicycle across the vast Place de la Concorde, staring at the long line of people straggling out of Paris towards the south.

Cars laden with furniture, mattresses strapped to the roofs, whole families jammed inside.

Men and women on bicycles, suitcases and bundles balanced precariously behind them. And the rest on foot, some pushing prams or leading reluctant animals behind them. Sheep. Goats.

An exodus.

EXT. OUTSIDE GOVERNMENT BUILDING — DAY

And now Suzie is passing a government building. She joins the curious

onlookers gathered behind the tall wrought-iron gates watching as boxes
of files are thrown from the windows and officials resignedly burn the
contents in a great bonfire in the courtyard.

INT. ON STAGE/AUDITORIUM — NIGHT

*Dante is peering out through a tiny gap in the stage curtains. A few
members of the orchestra are tuning up, muttering and murmuring dis-
tractedly.*

*Beyond them, the house is virtually empty. A few people straggle into
their seats and look around them at the desultory audience.*

Dante's face tightens with insecurity.

INT. DRESSING-ROOM — NIGHT

*Suzie stands alone in the empty dressing-room, usually so noisy and
crowded.*

*And then Felix Perlman appears in the doorway. She turns and looks
at him.*

                         SUZIE
   The show can't go on. There's nobody here.

But he shakes his head and points at her.

                         FELIX
   You're here.

INT. ON STAGE — NIGHT

*The opera (Il Trovatore by Verdi) is now in full swing, although with
less than half the usual orchestra.*

*Dante is singing. But there is something forced in his voice. He is trying
too hard, to compensate for the thin orchestral sound and the almost
empty house.*

Suzie appears alone at the back of the stage, the chorus of one.

*As Dante becomes aware of Suzie's voice joining in with his, exposed
and fully audible for the first time, he turns involuntarily, with a look
of surprise, towards her.*

INT. BACKSTAGE — NIGHT

*Suzie is hurrying across the deserted, darkened stage after the perform-
ance, when Dante stops her in her tracks.*

DANTE

You look more beautiful than before, Suzie.

SUZIE
(*politely*)

Why thank you, Dante.

DANTE

My mother was dark, like you.

He looks at her, carefully, appraisingly.

(*whispering*)

You have a good voice. I could help you.

SUZIE

But I don't need your help.

DANTE

Why do you resist me? What do you see in men who have
nothing?

Dante moves closer to Suzie. He starts to touch her hair.

(*softly*)

I like a girl with spirit. That's why you could become a somebody. Because you are a fighter, like me. We understand each
other. You have to fight to get somewhere in this world.
Maybe even fight to kill.

*He moves his face closer to hers, searching for her mouth, trying to kiss
her. But Suzie pulls away and looks Dante full in the face.*

SUZIE
(*quietly*)

If you are fighting to kill, you must be very, very sure that
you have God on your side, otherwise . . .

DANTE

Otherwise what?

SUZIE

. . . otherwise you are nothing more than a murderer.

Dante stares at her, and then abruptly drops his arm, and abandons his seductive manner.

DANTE
(*coldly*)
Let me tell you something about murderers. It was the Jews who killed Christ. The Jews.

Dante walks away from her, gesturing angrily, groping for words.

And this crazy war, which is caused by a conspiracy of . . . of . . . bankers . . . is stealing my public. I stand like a fool singing to an empty house.

He gestures wildly in the direction of the empty auditorium, and then turns back to Suzie. She does not look away. The more she stares at him, silently, with her implacable open gaze, the more Dante is trapped in an unstoppable, obsessive rage.

You think you are better than me. Right? You think that I am a peasant, an Italian peasant, and you are special, you are chosen. Well, let me remind you. Nobody knows what you are. Nobody *needs* to know, but you forget – I know, and I can –

FELIX
– I agree, Signor Dominio.

Felix Perlman steps out of the shadows, dressed, as usual, in his crumpled white linen suit. Dante wheels round to look at him.

No one needs to know . . . and no one needs to tell.

He looks at Dante and then at Suzie standing beside him, small and dark and silent.

Anyway, I came to tell you we're closing the production, which is sad for all of us.

DANTE
We're closing?

FELIX

Yes. Half the population of Paris has already left the city –

DANTE

– but my contract –

FELIX

– is meaningless, Dante. I have nothing left to give you. And, Dante – I must tell you – if Italy allies herself with Germany against France, then I am afraid your own position, as an Italian in Paris, will not be an enviable one.

DANTE

Is that a threat?

FELIX

A threat? From me? Dante – the Germans are in northern France heading for Paris, and my name is Perlman.

Dante stares at Felix for a moment and at Suzie, but then something takes his attention and he stalks off the stage. Cesar has appeared, silently, and is waiting for Suzie in the wings. She turns slowly to look at him.

EXT. STREETS – DAY

Dante looks pale and drawn as he climbs the steep steps towards the doors of a church.

INT. CHURCH – DAY

And then Dante is on his knees in the church in front of a statue of the Virgin Mary, staring up at her.

The statue – blonde, blue-eyed, blue-robed, pale-skinned, the baby Jesus in her arms – stares back down at him, ever compassionate, ever forgiving.

Dante's eyes fill with tears as he starts to pray.

DANTE

Oh, Maria . . .
What do I have but my voice, the voice that you gave me?
I am nothing if I cannot sing.
Oh, Maria, *Madre di Dio* . . .

For the love of Italy, for the love of music . . . I . . . I . . . I beg
you . . . let the Germans win.

INT. CHURCH — NIGHT

*Dante lies curled up on one of the pews in the church, red-eyed, broken
by exhaustion and discomfort.*

*Some other pews are occupied by people sitting and murmuring, pray-
ing through the night, a candle-lit vigil.*

Dante's eyes close.

INT. DANTE'S APARTMENT — NIGHT

*Lola paces about alone in the grand echoing apartment. She lights a
cigarette and stares gloomily into space.*

EXT. GYPSY ENCAMPMENT — DAWN

*Cesar is walking through the camp in the half-light of dawn towards
the horses' enclosure.*

*Cesar strokes his horse's mane and looks into its gleaming eyes. The
horse is restless and its ears are twitching back and forth, as if to some
unheard, distant, rhythmic sound.*

INT. SUZIE'S ROOM AND STAIRCASE — DAWN

Suzie's eyes open and she listens intently to a deep ominous rumble. And a rhythm. A relentless rhythm. She gets up from the bed, crosses the room and opens the windows, standing quietly in the early morning light.

The sound of feet, marching feet, faint, like a drumbeat, as the sun climbs above the rooftops.

INT. CHURCH — DAWN

Dante's eyes open as he lies crumpled and uncomfortable on the hard wooden pew. The first rays of daylight have penetrated the gloomy interior of the church.

And in the distance the unmistakable sound of feet, a huge army of marching feet, coming closer and closer.

INT. DANTE'S APARTMENT — DAY

Dante and Lola are sitting, motionless, on elegant upholstered chairs at opposite ends of the drawing-room.

The telephone rings, piercingly. Endlessly. Dante does not move. They stare at each other.

Eventually Lola gets up, crosses the room and picks up the phone.

> LOLA
> (*anxiously*)
> Hello?

EXT. CHÂTEAU AND GROUNDS — NIGHT

A group of Gypsy musicians are playing fast, frenetic music ('Tiganesca') in the grounds of the château. But their faces are stony and impassive as they play. Clearly, they are not playing for themselves. This is a job.

And the job is to play an accompaniment to the antics of those rich, drunken aristocrats who have remained in Paris after it has been occupied by the Germans.

But despite the noise and the brittle laughter, the atmosphere is tense and muted. The gathering is a pale echo of the party where Suzie and Lola had first met Dante and Cesar.

Cesar is leading a decorated donkey and trap back and forth as bejewelled women take it in turn to ride in the little cart, laughing hysterically at their own daring.

And collecting the coins that the revellers drop into a hat after their rides is none other than Suzie, her head lowered.

And then, suddenly, the crunch of wheels on gravel. Three shiny black cars sweep into the drive.

As they catch sight of the uniformed officers the Gypsies falter and fall silent one by one. But the hostess issues her instructions – whispered angrily to a servant – tell them to keep playing. And the servant scurries across the gravel and delivers his message, and the Gypsies reluctantly, woodenly, play on.

Suzie watches from a distance as the German officers in their unmistakable immaculate uniforms mingle politely with their French hosts. And there, amongst them, is Dante with the lovely Lola at his side.

She looks even more blonde than ever somehow; coiffed, groomed, powdered, a practised smile hovering on her perfectly made-up lips. Dante is wearing immaculate evening dress and is laughing, talking and gesturing expansively; perhaps too expansively.

A German officer is casting occasional admiring glances in Lola's direction. She gives him a little smile, enigmatic; but her attention is elsewhere. She has seen the young woman with lowered head working with the Gypsies at the far end of the grounds. Can it really be her?

GERMAN OFFICER

One must admit that these Gypsies can play their instruments well.

DANTE

Yes, but there is no control . . . no refinement of feeling . . .

FRENCH HOSTESS

Tell me, Dante, are you going to sing for us tonight?

                              DANTE
    Well . . . er . . .

*Dante coughs and puts a hand protectively to his throat. He is about to
answer, but the hostess has already turned to the German officer.*

                         FRENCH HOSTESS
    He sang for us all last year. But perhaps now he feels it is
    beneath his dignity – after his huge success.

Dante's jaw tightens at her sarcastic tone.
The hostess smiles viciously, playfully.

    He sang in Perlman's company.

                         GERMAN OFFICER
    Ah.

*She and the German officer raise their eyebrows at each other in mock
amusement.*
Dante is caught between their glances and tries his best to force a smile.

EXT. GYPSY ENCAMPMENT – NIGHT

*A contingent of German soldiers pulls up at the Gypsy encampment in
a car, several trucks following behind. The trucks are followed by small*

*excited children. The camp is deserted apart from some women and
children.*

*Soldiers jump out of the trucks and surge aggressively through the
camp towards the roped-off enclosure where the horses are kept.*

INT. CHÂTEAU — NIGHT

*Dante is now standing by a shiny grand piano and singing, accompa-
nied by one of the German officers. There is something forced, brittle, in
Dante's posture.*

*His eyes scan the faces of his listeners anxiously, particularly the faces
of the music-loving German officers.*

*And, yes, they are smiling, and listening attentively, as he sings a light,
popular, nostalgic, sentimental song ('Torna a Surriento'), the song of
a southern Italian longing for his home town.*

*Lola becomes aware of the German officer watching her appreciatively.
She turns and smiles, flirtatiously, but there is an emptiness in her
expression.*

Dante's soaring voice continues over . . .

EXT. GYPSY ENCAMPMENT — NIGHT

*. . . the German soldiers leading the horses, one by one, out of the
enclosure.*

*But the women and children are now fighting back, shouting and
pulling at the horses' reins. As the struggle becomes serious the soldiers
begin to get nasty.*

*A little boy tries to hold on to one of the horses. But then he is knocked
down. The horse panics. It rears up, its eyes rolling in alarm. The child
is trampled under its hooves.*

Screams. Mayhem. Chaos.

INT. CHÂTEAU — NIGHT

*Dante concludes his song and bows stiffly as the guests applaud appre-
ciatively.*

EXT. GROUNDS OF CHÂTEAU — NIGHT

Suzie is bent double with a little shovel, cleaning up the donkey's droppings in the grounds of the château.

And there, suddenly, is Dante, leaning over her, watching.

DANTE

Hey, little Suzie. So you have found your place at last, amongst the animals.

Suzie looks up at him. Looks into his smiling face, so pleased at his own witticism. Looks at the German officer standing at a distance, watching, as the lovely Lola waits silently in his shiny black car. Suzie slowly rises to her feet.

SUZIE

And you have found yours.

They stare at each other, as Dante realizes what Suzie is saying.

He turns, slowly, and strolls casually back towards the German officer and the waiting car.

GERMAN OFFICER

So you know the little girl, Dante?

Dante's face is blank. His eyes have become dead.

DANTE
(dully)

Oh, she was one of the . . . er . . . oddities employed by Perlman . . .

GERMAN OFFICER

Is she one of them?

DANTE

Although she is friendly with the Gypsies, she is not . . . one herself.

GERMAN OFFICER

Oh no? Then what is she?

Lola watches and listens, her immaculate powdered face an impenetra-

ble mask, as Dante hesitates, staring into the distance, as he struggles within himself, preparing to answer.

DANTE

She is a Jew.

EXT. GYPSY ENCAMPMENT — NIGHT

Cesar and the others arrive back at the camp to be met by screaming, weeping women and children.

The encampment is in uproar.
Cesar runs through the camp towards a group clustered around a little figure on the ground. The boy's father turns to face Cesar with an agonized expression, holding the child's broken body in his arms.

EXT. BRIDGE AND STREETS — DAY

The streets of Paris are now full of German soldiers, acting like tourists with their street maps and cameras, looking at the sights.

And that is how one of them, peering through the lens of the home-movie camera vibrating in his hand, sees two young women coming towards him across the bridge, one blonde, one dark.

The blonde smiles into his camera lens, flirtatiously, but the dark one turns her head away.

It is Lola and Suzie, walking the boulevards once more; boulevards now sign-posted in German and virtually empty of civilian cars, with a French population going about their business on bicycles or on foot.

LOLA

So many cameras! So many uniforms! Wherever I look there's a lens. I can't get away from them.

And then she leans towards Suzie and whispers conspiratorially.

Suzie, do you need anything? Meat? Butter? You know I can –

But Suzie interrupts her, coldly.

SUZIE

– Lola, what did you want to see me for?

71

Lola sighs and links her arm through Suzie's, who looks surprised at this sudden gesture of friendship.

LOLA

Ah, Suzie, I missed you! And I missed the fun we had together in our little room . . .

Then Lola's expression changes as she leads Suzie away from the crowds on the bridge and starts to speak in a small, quick, serious voice.

And, Suzie – I wanted to tell you, you should leave Paris. It's not safe for you here.

SUZIE

What do you mean?

Suzie stares at Lola questioningly, but Lola looks away.

LOLA

You should get out as soon as you can, that's all. Believe me.

And then she turns to Suzie with an innocent expression.

(*brightly*)

Look, suppose I . . . could get some tickets . . . some boat tickets to America, where you've always wanted to go.

SUZIE

I don't want to go there any more.

Suzie is staring coldly, implacably, at Lola. Lola drops her brightness like a stone.

LOLA

You do, Suzie, believe me. You absolutely do want to go. If you knew . . .

SUZIE

If I knew what?

Lola hovers, speechless for once, and then opens her handbag, flustered and breathless.

LOLA

Look, actually I've got the tickets right here in my bag. There's one for you . . . and there's one for me.

SUZIE

One for you? You're leaving Dante?

But Lola cannot hold Suzie's gaze. Her veneer is cracking. She turns away to hide her face.

LOLA
(*stumbling*)

Er . . . no. Not exactly . . .

SUZIE

He hasn't thrown you out?

LOLA

Don't be ridiculous, Suzie! I could have whatever I wanted. No, it's just that he . . . well, men . . . you can't trust them once they've got what they want. I should have known. It's dangerous to trust . . . well, actually, it's dangerous to love. Isn't that so, Suzie?

They stare at each other, silently, in acquiescence.

Anyway. One should never look back. One should never regret. Never.

And she smiles brightly once more at Suzie to recover her composure. They link arms and walk on.

EXT. ROAD NEAR GYPSY ENCAMPMENT — DAY

And now Suzie is walking beside Cesar at the end of a long procession of Gypsy mourners led by some musicians. Some pall-bearers are lurching through the mud, carrying a small lace-covered coffin. The women following the coffin are wailing.

Eventually Suzie glances up at Cesar and starts to speak.

SUZIE

They're planning to round everyone up. Every foreigner, every Jew. Lola says I should leave immediately. But I don't want to go.

They walk on in silence for a while.

If you want to survive, perhaps you have no choice.

Suzie turns and looks questioningly at Cesar.

INT. ROOM — NIGHT

Suzie is alone in her room, quietly packing her clothes into a small suit-case. She lays the tattered photograph of her father on top of her belongings.

And then there is a knock at the door and she freezes, and a flash of fear crosses her face. Already? They've come for me already?

But then she opens the door and Cesar is standing there, politely, holding a bottle of wine, waiting for the invitation to cross her threshold. She opens the door wide and he steps into the room he has never visited before.

Silence, as they gaze at each other. And then his eyes flicker to the photograph lying in the open suitcase. He reaches out and picks it up.

CESAR

Who is this?

SUZIE

It's my father.

He studies the faded, tattered photograph thoughtfully.

CESAR

A daughter should be with her father . . . if she is not with her husband.

Silence, again, as his words, politely uttered, fall into the air.

And then a choking, blind grief wells up in Suzie, the grief she has been holding inside her since her father left so long ago. And suddenly her pride snaps, and she reaches out and clings to Cesar.

SUZIE

Don't leave me, Cesar. Please don't go.

But she is begging him in the voice of a child, a confused and bereft little girl.

Cesar looks down at her, unafraid of her grief, knowing, somehow, that the grief is not really addressed to him.

CESAR

It is not me who is leaving, Suzie. It is you.

SUZIE

But I don't want to run away.

CESAR

For you, at this moment, running is good. It's better to run and live than to stay and die. It's not the same for me. I am not alone. I have my family.

As Suzie hears the implications of his words, she pulls away from him and crosses the room, wiping her eyes.

I must fight for my family.

SUZIE

I could stay and fight with you.

Cesar looks at Suzie with an open, honest look. They both know she's asking the impossible.

CESAR

You need to fight for yourself, Suzie.

SUZIE

But you're all I have.

Cesar gestures towards the photograph.

CESAR

No. You have your father.

SUZIE

If he's alive. Maybe I've been chasing a ghost.

Cesar crosses the room, opens the bottle of wine and pours it into two glasses.

CESAR

If he is a ghost . . . then he is watching over you. And if he is not . . . then he is waiting for you.

Suzie stares up at him.

And then they slowly raise their glasses of wine and toast each other.

To my Suzie, who will go to America, find her father . . . and sing.

SUZIE
(*softly*)
To my Cesar, who will stay . . . and fight for his family.

They each take a sip of wine and then slowly put their glasses down. Suzie gazes up into Cesar's face.

I only wish I could be with you . . .

But he smiles, touching her face softly for there are no words left. And then they kiss; tenderly, passionately.

Time has passed, and Suzie lies in Cesar's arms on the bed. Cesar, thinking her asleep, stares into the distance as he holds her, and softly starts to weep.

And now the long night has come to an end. Cesar appears to lie sleeping, at last. Suzie is now dressed. She quietly empties the jar of sugar into the sink. She retrieves the precious gold coin she has hidden there, crosses the room, and puts it gently, lovingly, like an offering, into Cesar's pocket.

Then she picks up her suitcase and stands at the door, looking at Cesar one last time before stepping out and closing the door gently behind her.

Cesar opens his eyes and stares into the empty silence in the room.

EXT. HARBOUR — NIGHT

And so it is that Suzie finds herself, eventually, side-by-side with Lola in the back of a small boat, setting out across the choppy dark water in a harbour.

But although they are sitting in the same boat, they may as well be in different worlds.

Lola's usually immaculate appearance has taken a battering on the journey south, but her eyes are bright and eagerly focused on the ocean liner anchored in the distance, its lights reflected on the water.

But Suzie's eyes are full and dark as she looks back through the white foaming spray in the wake of the little boat as it leaves the protection of the harbour, thinking of what she's leaving behind.

INT. SHIP CABIN — NIGHT

Suzie and Lola are lying silently, exhausted, in their cabin, as the large ship's anchor is hauled up through the water. Once again the two women have narrow beds on opposite sides of a tiny space.

INT. SHIP RESTAURANT — NIGHT

Suzie is standing on a small stage in the ship's restaurant.

She is singing a melancholy, popular song ('Gloomy Sunday') that will distract the anxious passengers and help to keep the terrors of war at bay.

Sitting at a table, quietly watching her and listening, is Lola.

But when Suzie sings, accompanied by the small ship's band, it's not just Lola but most of the tense and restless passengers who pause for a moment, forks suspended in mid-air, to listen to this dark-eyed girl, soothed and fortified by her lovely voice; a voice that somehow transforms the song they thought they knew into something else, something resembling a prayer.

But then an elegant, older man indicates the empty seat next to Lola and silently asks his permission to join her. She looks up at him for a long moment and then gestures for him to sit down.

Suzie's song continues over, as . . .

EXT. ON DECK – NIGHT

. . . later that night, Suzie and Lola meet on deck and Lola speaks to Suzie in a bright, cheery voice.

LOLA

Frankly, Suzie, Joe is a little older than I like, but . . . you

know what? He has promised to help me – and you – get to
Hollywood. You see? Things always turn out for the best.

                    SUZIE
                   (*quietly*)
Do they?

*An awkward silence falls between the two women. Lola studies Suzie's
face, searching for the right words, a conciliatory gesture, anything.*

                    LOLA
                   (*softly*)
And your father, Suzie. That will be nice for you, to see him
at last, yes?

                    SUZIE
Yes. Perhaps.

                    LOLA
                   (*brightly*)
Anyway, we have each other again. We can have *fun*. We can
forget all those little differences, can't we, Suzie? Yes?

They look at each other and Lola smiles, brightly, bravely. And needily.

*Suzie's expression softens and she smiles, sadly but reassuringly, at
Lola.*

INT. SWIMMING POOL – NIGHT

*Lola is standing alone by the edge of a deserted art-nouveau,
Romanesque-style swimming pool, deep in the hull of the ship, a swimming cap covering her blonde hair, her face bare and vulnerable, her
expression unguarded for once as she contemplates the water, unobserved.*

EXT. ON DECK – NIGHT

*Suzie is standing alone on deck, sheltering from the wind and rain,
staring at the photograph of her father. She puts it back in her pocket.
And then the low rumble of the ship's engines is joined by another
growling, whining sound. A sound that comes from the sky and gets
closer and closer. Suzie looks up, suddenly, in alarm, as she realizes
what she is seeing . . .*

INT. SWIMMING POOL — NIGHT

... Lola is floating, curled foetus-like in the turquoise water of the swimming pool, oblivious.

Suddenly there is a horrible muffled thud, followed by a short but endless silence. And then a blinding explosion.

The boat lurches violently in the aftershock, as the water in the pool surges and Lola is picked up and dashed against the edge of the pool ...

EXT. THE SEA — NIGHT

... the explosion has hurled Suzie into the dark sea-water. But she surfaces, gasping for breath, a seething inferno of fire on the surface of the water all around her.

EXT. THE SEA AND SMALL BOAT — NIGHT

And now Suzie is being hauled out of the water by some sailors and laid down in the bottom of a small boat, and they are pumping water out of her lungs as she lies face down, barely conscious.

INT. SALOON IN TRAMP STEAMER — DAY

Suzie stands gazing out from behind a window on the deck of the small tramp steamer that had rescued her as it limps into New York City in the early hours of a grey and misty morning.

The ghostly reflections of the city skyline ripple across Suzie's face. Pale, bereft, alone. Once again she is the lonely survivor on her journey.

INT. JEWISH REFUGEE ORGANIZATION — DAY

A relief-worker is holding the remains of the photograph of Suzie's father in her hands in a busy, crowded office.

> RELIEF-WORKER
> I'm pretty sure it's on the border with Russia. Sit.

She gestures to a chair next to a desk piled with papers, then crosses the room and starts rifling through a filing cabinet, occasionally glancing down at the blurred name and address on the scrap of paper.

> Let me check the files from that region. You know what? You're lucky you had an English passport. The quotas from so many East European countries are full now. You wouldn't believe the stories I've heard. America is a big country, but not big enough to take all of *us*, apparently. But we should be able to trace someone who remembers him.

INT. SWEATSHOP — DAY

And now Suzie is standing with the relief-worker from the refugee organization in a corner of a crowded, noisy, steamy sweatshop.

An older man, wearing a long shabby dark coat, stares at the barely visible name on the back of the scrap of photo in his hands, and speaks to Suzie in a cautious, solicitous tone of voice.

> OLDER MAN
> Abramovitch. Yes . . . I think I know of this man.

He shakes his head meaningfully.

A group is slowly gathering around them, peering at the scrap of photo and at Suzie. Suzie looks at the faces gazing at her with pity and with guilty relief that they are amongst the survivors of this and other even more terrible tragedies of separation, of death, of disaster.

Suzie stares at them, blankly.

> SECOND MAN
> – but wait a minute. Isn't it the guy, who . . . er . . . lost his faith?

> THIRD MAN
> Yes, that's the one!

> SECOND MAN
> It has to be –

> THIN WOMAN
> – what a voice! –

The older man silences the group clustered around them.

> OLDER MAN
> – please, please. He said he had heard that the shtetl where he had left his mother and his daughter had been burned to the ground and everyone perished. Everyone! He said that he could no longer believe in a just God and therefore could no longer sing.

> THIN WOMAN
> It was a scandal. Everybody talked about it.

> THIRD MAN
> Everybody, everybody!

Suzie stares at them.

> SUZIE
> But what happened to him?

> OLDER MAN
> He changed his name along with his profession and went west.

> THIRD MAN
> *(sighing)*
> Yes, it was a terrible thing. The man was a chazan, a religious man.

THIN WOMAN

But he did well, you must admit, he did very well.

FOURTH MAN

Listen. If you have a vision, and you work hard like him, you can succeed over here.

EXT. HOLLYWOOD STUDIO — DAY

Suzie is standing on the back lot of a film studio, looking about her at the painted sets of American cities, the men dressed as cowboys, at the automobiles and trailers and signs of money, money everywhere.

Eventually she manages to get the attention of one of the bronzed assistants dashing about carrying a clipboard.

SUZIE

Excuse me! Do you know where I can find Mr Abrahams?

BRONZED ASSISTANT

Why would my boss want to speak to you?

SUZIE

Well, he's my father.

BRONZED ASSISTANT

Your father!

He looks at her in disbelief. But then something in her eyes makes him relent.

I think I'd better take you to our legal department. Follow me.

INT. OFFICE — DAY

Suzie is sitting opposite a lawyer on the other side of a vast desk.

SUZIE
(*quietly*)

I'd like to see my father, that's all.

LAWYER

As you keep saying. And, if that's who he really is, then you will see him.

84

He stares at her and at the battered photo she has given him, and then at one of the many photographs sitting on his desk. It's a photograph in a heavy silver frame of a tall thin man, a blonde woman by his side, his hands resting on the shoulders of two blonde, freckly children standing in front of them. Could this be the same man?

Perhaps the man in the photograph on his desk does resemble this quiet, insistent girl who now sits staring at him across the desk . . . something in the eyes . . .

But he is not well, you understand, not well at all. His musicals have eaten him alive. Frankly, he has worn himself out. His family is very upset. Very upset.

SUZIE

He has a family?

INT. HOSPITAL — DAY

And so Suzie finds herself at last following a nurse down a long, blindingly white hospital corridor.

And she walks and walks, taking the last steps on her long and broken journey, faltering only at the very end as she pauses briefly outside an open door.

Standing to one side of the door is the blonde woman from the photo and the two freckly, all-American children, a boy and a girl. They stare at the dark stranger as she approaches; a ghost from the past . . .

INT. HOSPITAL ROOM — DAY

And then a nurse steps aside and Suzie sees him.
A thin man, lying very still, under the starched white covers in the immaculate, sterile room. He looks at her. She looks at him.

And then slowly Suzie crosses the room and stands by the bed, the young healthy woman looking down at the exhausted man. He gazes up at her, immobile, unblinking.

FATHER
(*whispering*)

Fegele . . .

SUZIE
(*whispering*)

Tateh . . .

FATHER
(*whispering*)

Fegele . . .
My little . . . bird.

And then something turns in her, and time itself suddenly seems to slow down and she finds herself reaching out to him through her tears.

She sits on the bed, takes his hand and kisses it, and then starts to sing to him, softly, in Yiddish, the lullaby he had once sung to her as a child.

SUZIE
(*singing in Yiddish*)

Close your eyes
And you shall go
To that sweet land
All dreamers know

Where milk and honey
Always flow
Rest now, Papa
You can go.

And as he listens to her sing, the guilt and sorrow in his face slowly melt and his eyes fill with tears.

And for Suzie, in this moment of hearing her real name, Fegele, and remembering her language, she realizes not only what she has irrevocably lost, but also what it is that she has become. The voice she is hearing is, at last, not her father's, but her own. And it is her turn, now, to comfort, to soothe and to be strong.

A tiredness washes over her father's face as she sings. He closes his eyes. For a moment it seems that he is slipping away from her and slipping away from life itself.

But then he looks up at her – a look of love – and she smiles at him, forgiving, grateful, glowing. They are both survivors.

86

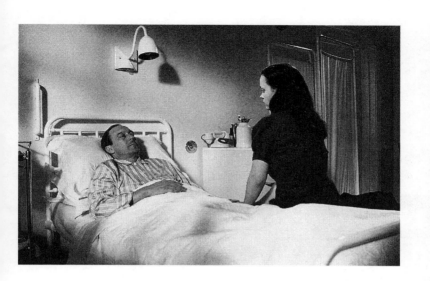

CREDITS

STUDIOCANAL & UNIVERSAL PICTURES
present
a WORKING TITLE production
in association with
ADVENTURE PICTURES

a SALLY POTTER film

THE MAN WHO CRIED

Casting by
IRENE LAMB
US casting by
MARY COLQUHOUN
Original music score by
OSVALDO GOLIJOV
Production Designer
CARLOS CONTI
Costume Designer
LINDY HEMMING
Editor
HERVE SCHNEID A.C.E.
Director of Photography
SACHA VIERNY
Co-producer
SIMONA BENZAKEIN
Executive Producers
TIM BEVAN
ERIC FELLNER
Producer
CHRISTOPHER SHEPPARD
Written and directed by
SALLY POTTER

(in order of appearance)

Suzie	CHRISTINA RICCI
Father	OLEG YANKOVSKIY
Young Suzie	CLAUDIA LANDER-DUKE
Man in Suit	DANNY SCHEINMANN
Mother of Man in Suit	ANNA TZELNIKER
Men in Village	BARRY DAVIS
	THOM OSBORN
	FRANK CHERSKY
	DANIEL HART
	PETER MAJER
Grandmother	HANA MARIA PRAVDA
Children	AYALA MEIR
	ABRAHAM HASSAN
	LLOYD MARTIN
	URI MEIR
	SOPHIE RICHMAN
	THEO WISHART
Boys in Cart	MICHAEL MOUNT
	HARRY FLINDER
Man in Cart	DANNY RICHMAN
Man at Port	VICTOR SOBTCHAK
Red Cross Woman	SUE CLEAVER
English Port Official	CLIFFORD BARRY
Second Official	PAUL CLAYTON
Foster Mother	DIANA HODDINOTT
Foster Father	RICHARD ALBRECHT
Playground Bullies	ORNELLA BRYANT
	SAM FRIEND
	ISABELLA MELLING
Welsh Teacher	ALAN DAVID
Audition Mistress	IMOGEN CLAIRE
Lola	CATE BLANCHETT
Madame Goldstein	MIRIAM KARLIN
Cesar	JOHNNY DEPP
Party Hostess	CONSUELO DE HAVILAND
Felix Perlman	HARRY DEAN STANTON
Dante Dominio	JOHN TURTURRO
Pianists	KATIA LABEQUE
	MARIELLE LABEQUE
Reporter	GEORGE YIASOUMI

Dancing Romany	PABLO VERON
Romany Band	TARAF DE HAÏDOUKS
Opera Chorus	ODILE ROIRE
	BRIGITTE BOUCHER
	NORAH KRIEF
	HELENE HARDOUIN
Romany Brothers	HUGUES DALMAGRO
	CEDRIC GARY
Romany Boy	SAIFI GHOUL
German Officer	MANFRED ANDRAE
German Officer Pianist	RICHARD SAMMEL
Father of Boy	AHMET ZIREK
Joe	DON FELLOWS
Refugee Worker	JOYCE SPRINGER
Older Man in Sweatshop	CYRIL SHAPS
Woman in Sweatshop	ANNA KORWIN
Men in Sweatshop	MARK IVANIR
	ALFRED HOFFMAN
	BERNARD SPEAR
Studio Assistant	DAMIEN PUCKLER
Studio Lawyer	DAVID BAXT
Father's New Wife	KATHERINE HOGARTH
Son	PATRICK CLARKE
Daughter	BRIDGET CLARKE
Nurse	CHRIS GILLESPIE

CREW

Line Producer	LINDA BRUCE
First Assistant Directors	CHRIS NEWMAN
	JEROME BORENSTEIN
Story Editor	WALTER DONOHUE
Script Supervisor	PENNY EYLES
Sound Mixer	JEAN-PAUL MUGEL
Camera Operator	YVES VANDERMEEREN
Location Managers	MARC GUIDETTI
	BILL DARBY
Financial Controller	KEVIN TREHY
Chief Make-up Designer	MORAG ROSS
Chief Hair Designer	JAN ARCHIBALD
Production Managers	PATRICK MILLET
	RACHEL NEALE
Music Editor	ANDY GLEN

Supervising Sound Editor	EDDY JOSEPH
Post-production Supervisor	JEANETTE HALEY

FOR WORKING TITLE

Chief Operating Officer	ANGELA MORRISON
Head of Business Affairs	RACHEL HOLROYD
Executive in Charge of Production	MICHELLE WRIGHT
Focus Puller	JEAN-PIERRE SUPE
Loader	CAROLE TIZON
Key Grip	ANDRE HAIDANT
Camera Trainee	FRANCOIS LE GOFF
Boom Operator	SOPHIE CHIABAUT
Sound Assistants	STEPHANE SOYE
	PETER COWAJJI
Production Manager for Adventure Pictures	MICHAEL MANZI
Production Co-ordinators	ROANNE MOORE
	FLORENCE FORNEY
Line Producer Services France	PIE
Assistant to Sally Potter	AMOS FIELD REID
Assistant to Tim Bevan	JULIETTE DOW
Assistant to Eric Fellner	LARA THOMPSON
Company Co-ordinator for Working Title	NINA KHOSHABA
Head of Finance for Working Title	JULIAN TOMLIN
Legal Services	DIANE GELON
Choreographer	JACKY LANSLEY
Choreographer (Romany Café)	PABLO VERON
Casting Director	FREDERIQUE MOIDON
Second Assistant Director	BEN HOWARTH
Third Assistant Director	JANET NIELSEN
Steadicam Operators	VALENTIN MONGE
	KATE ROBINSON
Steadicam Loader	SHAUN COBLEY
Steadicam Focus Pullers	SEBASTIEN LECLERCQ
	LUKE REDGRAVE
Second Unit Operator	JEAN-PIERRE HERVE
Second Unit Loaders	VINCENT PLAIDY
	IAN COFFEY
Third Unit Camera Operator	STEVE HALL
Third Unit Focus Puller	BRAD LARNER

Underwater Cameraman	MIKE VALENTINE BSC
Underwater Focus Puller	DEAN MORRISH
Underwater Loader	JAMES SCOTT
Underwater Camera Assistant	GRIETJE BESTERMAN
Production Administrator	CHANTAL MALRAT-ATANASSIAN
Accountants	LISA-KIM LING KUAN
	ALAIN DOMINIECKI
Assistant Accountants	JOSEPHINE OLIVE-O'NEILL
	BETTY AINSLIE
Grips	GERARD HAIDANT
	MARC CASI
	JEAN-PIERRE GESBERT
	FABRICE BOURDERIOUX
	CYRILLE PIERRON
Third Unit Grip	JIM CROWTHER
Extras Handlers	ELODIE MORALES
	SEBASTIEN DARBOIS
Crowd Assistant Director	SUSAN WOOD
Assistant Location Managers	FREDERIC SOBCZAK
	DUNCAN FLOWER
Location Scouts	XAVIER-DAVID BENKEMOUN
	EMMANUEL RONDEAU DU NOYER
	EMMANUEL ROUSSILLE
Location Assistants	SAMANTHA THOMAS
	BRIDGET KENNINGHAM
Location Trainees	SONIA DUCLOS
	LUDOVIC BEURTON
	EMMANUEL LIBERMANN
	MATHIEU HILTZER
	MARC LE CAMPION
Extras Casting Director	ANDREAS MESZAROS
Romany Casting Director	ANNICK HEMON
Assistant Casting Directors	IRIS WONG
	HELENE PAUTRE
	LUCY TOWNSEND
Romany Liaison	FELICIA BANU
Taraf de Haïdouks Management	MICHEL WINTER
	STEPHANE KARO
Dialect Coach	BARBARA BERKERY
Historical Advisor	MARIE-PIERRE THOMAS
Yiddish Advisor	BARRY DAVIS
Romany Consultants	ISABEL FONSECA

	DONALD KENRICK
Lip-synching Consultant	DANIEL LIPNIK
Opera Singer Coach	JANE ROBINSON
Russian Interpreter	NINA KHOBIASHVILI
First Assistant Editors	SIMON COZENS
	ISABELLE PROUST
Second Assistant Editors	TANIA CLARKE
	NATASHA PYM
Dialogue Editor	NICK LOWE A.M.P.S.
Foley Editor	PETER HOLT
Assistant Sound Editors	RICHARD FORDHAM
	STEVE MAYER
	ALEX JOSEPH
Assistant Music Editors	SOPHIE CORNET
	TONY LEWIS
	MATTHEW BARR
Re-recording Mixers	ROBIN O'DONOGHUE
	and DOMINIC LESTER
Assisted by	RICHARD STREET
	and NIGEL BENNETT
Foley Mixer	ED COLYER
Assisted by	DAVID TYLER
ADR Voice Casting	LOUIS ELMAN
	ALTER EGO
Foley Artists	PAULINE GRIFFITHS
	RICKY BUTT
Re-recorded at	SHEPPERTON FILM STUDIOS,
	ENGLAND
Post-production Consultancy	STEEPLE POST PRODUCTION SERVICES
Additional Make-up and Hair to Christina Ricci	ELIZABETH TAGG
Make-up Artist to Johnny Depp	NATHALIE TISSIER
Make-up Artists	CHANTAL LEOTHIER
	SYLVIE LONCHAMP
	KARINA GRUAIS
	MELISSA LACKERSTEEN
Chief Hairstylist	BEYA GASMI
Hairdressers	ANITA BURGER
	REYNALD DESBANT
	GERARD CARRISSIMOUX
	LOULIA SHEPPARD
Wardrobe Supervisor	DAVID CROSSMAN

First Costume Design Assistant	JACQUELINE DURRAN
Assistant Costume Designers	DANY EVERETT
	CARIN HOFF
	GUY SPERANZA
Breakdown Artist	TIM SHANAHAN
Wardrobe Mistress	KAREN MULLER-SERREAU
Artist Dressers	VERONIQUE PORTEBOIS
	SANDRINE DOUAT
Wardrobe Assistants	ANDREA CRIPPS
	VICKY CLARK
	AMANDA DERBY
Dressers	ERIC BIGOT
	JANET FIONA LATIMER
	SEBASTIAN PERRONE
	JACQUES MAZUEL
Runner/Drivers	NICOLAS PLOUX
	DAVID CRENN
Art Directors	LAURENT OTT
	BEN SCOTT
Assistant Art Director	MATTHEW GRAY
Second Assistant Art Directors	STEPHANE CRESSEND
	BETTINA VON DEN STEINEN
	MARIANNA ZENTCHENKO
Draughtsman	AL BULLOCK
Art Department Assistants	ANDREA MATHESON
	ALEX DURY
Art Department Trainee	ROMAN TURLURE
Set Decorators	PHILIPPE TURLURE
	MAGGIE GRAY
Production Buyer	LUCINDA STURGIS
Props Buyer	JACQUES QUINTERNET
Assistant Props Buyer	ARNAUD PUTMAN
Head Draper	JACQUES KAZANDJIAN
Draper Trainees	STEPHANE FORTIER-DURAND
	CAROLINE PLATIAU
	ADELINE PRAIZNER
Props Master	GRAEME PURDY
Supervising Propman	BRUCE BIGG
Dressing Props	PIERRE BANDINI
	PETER BIGG
	NICHOLAS MILNER
Chargehand Dressing Props	STEVE PAYNE

Assistant Dressing Props	FRANCOIS BARRE
	JACQUES MOISSINAC
	GREGORY ECK
	MIGUEL NOUGIER
Vehicle Consultant	MARTIN GRANGE
Storeman	SULAIMAN MALCOLM BENSTED
Props Trainee	JASON HOPPERTON
Chargehand Standby Props	OLIVIER CRESPIN
	ROBERT SHERWOOD
Standby Props	BRUNO HADJADJ
	BILLY HARGREAVES
Construction Managers	PATRICK WIDDRINGTON
	BERNARD BOIVIN
	DAVE BUBB
Standby Carpenter	ALLEN PACK
Standby Painter	PETER HAMMOND
Standby Rigger	STEVE SANSOM
Standby Stagehand	JAMES MUIR
Head Carpenters	ROGER SAILLARD
	IGOR MOLLET
	LEON APSEY

Carpenters

Karl Apsey, Dennis Bovington, Alan P. Brooks, Lionel Christian, Daniel Clereci, Jean Dambrin, Patrick Delmas, Lee Edwards, Eric Frion, David Gibson, Jonathan Godfrey, Christian Guillebaut, Pascal Guyot, Brian Higgins, Michael Law, Albert Long, Jerome Magne, Wolfgang Oster-holzer, Michael Simpson, Michael Traynor, Barry Weller, Dean Weller

Wood Machinist	STEPHEN WESTON
Head Painter	DANIEL MAUVIGNIER
Supervising Scenic Painter	JOHN DAVEY
Scenic Painter	DEAN DUNHAM
Sculptors	ISABELLE GLOBENSKY
	JEAN WIRTH
	YANN HAUGOMAT
	ANNE DOLET

Painters

David Carter, Guy Chouard, Ronald Fallen, Christian Giambiasi, Bertrand Guinnebault, Jean-Francois Juvanon, Yannis Kyroglou, Ronald Lattimore, Patrick Lepetit, Gary McCarthy, Kevin McCarthy, Laurent Micheletti, Stanislas Robiolle, Paul Whitelock

Letter Painter	ALBA PONCE
Riggers	KEITH BATTERBEE

	JAMES KNOX
Chargehand–Stagehand	KEITH MUIR
Stagehands	PETER WELLS
	MICHAEL DRISCOLL
	PHILIP MORRIS
Locksmiths	JEAN LABILLE
	FRANCIS LEBRUN
Gaffer	JEAN-CLAUDE LEBRAS
Best Boys	ALAIN DONDIN
	ROLAND DONDIN
	RONNIE PHILLIPS
Electricians	STEPHANE CRY
	DAVID ESCOFFERY
	TONY HANNINGTON
Generator Operators	PHILIPPE GUERMOUTH
	BARRY BILOTTI
Practical Electricians	MARK DIJKMEIJER
	JOHN MELVILLE
Rigging Electrician	TONY CARDENAS
Production Assistant	AARON DE LUCA
Assistant to Christina Ricci	KATE JONES
Production Runner	HARVEY WALLER
Floor Runners	FRANCOIS BELL
	PIERRE TURQUET
	DATHI SVEINBJARNARSON
Special Effects	ALAIN COUTY
	OLIVIER ZENENSKI
Special Effects Supervisor	DOMINIC TUOHY
Special Effects Assistant	JEM LOVETT
Horse Master	MARIO LURASCHI
Stunt Co-ordinators	JOELLE BALLAND
	PASCAL 'CHINO' MADURA
	ANDY BRADFORD
Stunt Double for Johnny Depp	LAURENT ALEXANDRE
Stunt Performers	DAVID ANDERS
	RICHARD BRADSHAW
	GARY CONNERY
	GABE CRONNELLY
	DEREK LEA
Driving Double	JIM LOCKWOOD
Unit Publicist	ALEXIS DELAGE-TORIEL
Stills Photographer	PETER MOUNTAIN

Stand-ins for Christina Ricci	FLORENCE GRUNFELDER
	HELEN SLAYMAKER
Stand-in for Johnny Depp	SEBASTIEN JACQUET
Stand-ins for Cate Blanchett	MIREILLE WOZNY
	COLETTE APPLEBY
Stand-in for John Turturro	XAVIER MENUT
Stand-in for Harry Dean Stanton	DOMINIQUE SELLIER
Stand-in for Claudia Lander-Duke	LINDSEY MUSE
Stand-in for Oleg Yankovskiy	ALEX ALEXANDER
Utility Stand-ins	FABIO CARDASCIA
	JOHN BARTRAM
	KAREN HALLIDAY
Health and Safety Officers	CYRIL GIBBONS
	DOUGLAS YATES
Nurses	SOPHIE MOLLIER
	NICOLA GREGORY JARVIS
Underwater Communications Nurse	FRANCOISE VALENTINE
Transport Managers	LAURENT RIZZON
	DAVE MANNING

Drivers

Felix Baudouin, Mathias Bocquillon, Helene Chalant, Fred Chiverton, Mick Crowley, Colin Davies, Stephane Floc'h, Yahn Jeannot, Paul Jones, Philip Knight, Pascal LeGrand, Jerry O'Connor, Ken Price, Bob Sachs, Marc-Antoine Trani, Gerry Turner, RJ Turner

Completion Guarantee provided by	INTERNATIONAL FILM GUARANTORS, INC.
Insurance	AON/ALBERT G. RUBEN

Digital Colour and Visual Effects by
DUBOICOLOR

Technical Director	RIP HAMPTON O'NEIL
Production Manager	TOMMASO VERGALLO
Digital Colour Grader	CLAIRE COUTELLE
Digital Scan Supervisor	CHRISTOPHE BELENA
Scan Assistant	CORALIE BOULAY
Special Effects Production Manager	EDOUARD VALTON
Special Effects Supervisor	MARCO PACCOSI
Special Effects Project Supervisor	SEVERINE DE WEVER
Dutruc Operators	ANDRE BRIZARD
	THIERRY DELOBEL

	STEPHANE DITOO
	ANTOINE LHOUILLER
	JEAN-FRANCOIS MICHELAS
	SEBASTIEN RAME
	DANIEL TRUJILLO
Matador Operators	SOLEN COLLIGNON
	ALEXANDRE KOLASINSKI
Digital Title Designer	VERONIQUE ZYLBERFAIN
Digital Transfer	FRANCOIS DUPUY
	ALEXANDRE JEANNERET
	TINA LIN
Chief Executive Officer	ANTOINE SIMKINE
Cameras and Lenses by	IRIS CAMERA
Laboratories	LABORATOIRE ECLAIR
	TECHNICOLOR
Colour Timing	YVAN LUCAS
	PHIL ASHTON
Negative Cutting	SYLVIA WHEELER FILM SERVICES
Dolby Sound Consultant	JAMES SEDDON
Special Effects	EFFECTS ASSOCIATES
CGI	DOUBLE NEGATIVE
Graphics Consultant	STEVE MASTERS
Costumiers	ANGELS COSTUMES
	COSPROP
Catering	CINE FOOD
	SET MEALS
Stills Processing	CENTRAL COLOR
	BLOWUP
Editing Equipment	VIRTUEL 24/25
Editing Facilities	ARTISTIC PALACE
	MIDNIGHT TRANSFER
Sound Archive News Recording licensed by	BBC WORLDWIDE

Soundtrack available exclusively on SONY CLASSICAL

Original Score performed by
KRONOS QUARTET

with
Guitars	FRED FRITH
Double Bass	CHRISTOPHER LAURENCE

Music Producer	SALLY POTTER
Executive Music Producer	CHRISTOPHER SHEPPARD
Opera Music Producer	DAVID FROST
Opera Music Conductor	SIAN EDWARDS
Music Recorded and Mixed by	MIKE ROSS-TREVOR
Music Co-ordinator for Adventure Pictures	AMOS FIELD REID
Music Management and Supervision	MUSICALITIES LIMITED
Music Supervisor	IVAN CHANDLER
Music Co-ordinator	JENNY TOOK
Music Licensing Consultant	JILL MEYERS
Music Copying/Preparation	GLOBAL MUSIC SERVICE
Music Consultant to Mr Golijov	ROBERT THOMPSON

JE CROIS ENTENDRE ENCORE ('Yiddish version'), from *The Pearl Fishers* by Georges Bizet. Performed by Salvatore Licitra and the Orchestra of the Royal Opera House. Concertmaster: Vasko Vassilev.

DIDO'S LAMENT, from *Dido and Aeneas* by Henry Purcell. Performed by Iva Bittova, piano accompaniment by Dave Arch.

JE CROIS ENTENDRE ENCORE, from *The Pearl Fishers* by Georges Bizet. Performed by Salvatore Licitra, piano accompaniment by Katia Labeque and Marielle Labeque.

BANGI KHELIMOS. Composed by Sapo Perapaskero, performed by Taraf de Haïdouks. Courtesy of Crammed Discs.

DUCHO BALVALO. Composed by Sapo Perapaskero, performed by Taraf de Haïdouks. Courtesy of Crammed Discs.

DIDO'S LAMENT, from *Dido and Aeneas* by Henry Purcell. Performed by Iva Bittova and Taraf de Haïdouks. Courtesy of Crammed Discs.

JE CROIS ENTENDRE ENCORE, from *The Pearl Fishers* by Georges Bizet. Performed by Salvatore Licitra and the Orchestra of the Royal Opera House. Concertmaster: Vasko Vassilev.

TORNA A SURRIENTO. Written by E. De Curtis, G. B. De Curtis (E. De Curtis, G. B. De Curtis, A. Mazzucchi for USA and Canada), performed by Salvatore Licitra, piano accompaniment by Katia Labeque.

GLOOMY SUNDAY. Written by Rezsoe Seress, Laszlo Javor and Desmond Carter, arranged by Steve Prutsman, performed by Iva Bittova, accompanied by Brian Dee, Andrew Cleyndert and Clarke Tracey.

CLOSE YOUR EYES. Composed by Osvaldo Golijov, lyrics by Sally Potter, performed by Salvatore Licitra.

JALOUSIE. Written by Gade/May, performed by Pamela Nicholson and Vasko Vassilev.

DI QUELLA PIRA, from *Il Trovatore* by Guiseppe Verdi. Performed by Salvatore Licitra and Iva Bittova with the Orchestra of the Royal Opera House, Concertmaster: Vasko Vassilev. The Royal Opera Chorus, Chorus Director: Terry Edwards.

GLOOMY SUNDAY. Written by Rezsoe Seress, Laszlo Javor and Desmond Carter, performed by Kronos Quartet. Courtesy of Nonesuch Records, by arrangement with Warner Special Products/Warner UK Strategic Marketing.

BALADELE REVOLUTEII. Composed by Sapo Perapaskero, performed by Taraf de Haïdouks. Courtesy of Crammed Discs.

E LUCEVAN LE STELLE, from *Tosca* by Giacomo Puccini. Performed by Salvatore Licitra with the Orchestra of the Royal Opera House, Concertmaster: Vasko Vassilev.

TIGANESCA. Composed by Sapo Perapaskero, performed by Taraf de Haïdouks. Courtesy of Crammed Discs.

CHALARIMASTAR TE BISTRAW. Composed by Sapo Perapaskero, performed by Taraf de Haïdouks. Courtesy of Crammed Discs.

CLOSE YOUR EYES. Composed by Osvaldo Golijov, lyrics by Sally Potter, performed by Iva Bittova.

In loving memory of Betty Mary Sheppard

Special thanks to:
Diane Balser, Alexandra Cann, Julie Christie, Adrienne Clarkson, Robyn Davidson, Peter Gelb, Dominique Green, Mark Halloran, Julian Henriques, Charles Moore, Simon Perry, Hugh Rolo, Tony Safford, Pierre Selinger, Parminder Vir, Bart Walker

Mairie de Paris – Madame Brigitte Brauner
Prefecture de Police de Paris
Eclairage de la Tour Eiffel – Copyright Societe Nouvelle d'Exploitation de la Tour Eiffel
France-Rail Publicité – Monsieur Jean-Pierre Haubensack
La Gendarmerie Nationale, Euro-Signal Distribution, France Telecom,

L'A.S.A.V., Jewish Music Distribution, Forest Enterprise Bourne Wood,
The RAC Club

DOLBY DIGITAL in selected theatres
SONY DYNAMIC DIGITAL SOUND in selected theatres
DTS DIGITAL SOUND in selected theatres

Originated on Motion Picture Film supplied by KODAK
Motion Picture Association of America No. 37649
Developed with the assistance of British Screen Finance Limited,
London, England